My Breaking Point, God's Turning Point

My Breaking Point, God's Turning Point is a brilliant and insightful look into the ability to triumph over tragedy. It's a must-read for all. Ricky has a wonderful writing style that welcomes his readers into the family. This book will strengthen you, encourage you and, simply put, "make you feel like you can win again." It's a home-run experience for your heart.

Gordon Banks
Senior Pastor, Overcomer Covenant Church, Seattle, Washington
Former NFL Player, Dallas Cowboys

The redemptive story of Ricky and Cyd Texada has challenged me to realize that God is sovereignly in charge of even the disappointments of life. God has worked a miracle and has thrust the Texadas into a fruitful ministry after devastating disappointment. If God can bring together such a "dynamic duo" from the brink of devastation, what can He do for you to turn your "mourning into joy"? Read this book and let God open a new window of opportunity in your heart: *The best is yet to come!*

Larry Stockstill
Director, Surge Project
Pastor Emeritus, Bethany Church, Baton Rouge, Louisiana

Richard Exley once said, "I want to read books that sing." He would love this book; it sings almost every kind of genre and then some. I've known Pastors Ricky and Cyd Texada for two decades, only to discover in reading his story—I didn't know him at all! There are songs in this book for weeping and songs for rejoicing. You'll do both as I did.

Joseph L. Garlington, Sr.
Presiding Bishop, Covenant Church of Pittsburgh

This book will inspire you to believe that God can and will work all things out for those who love Him. It is filled with hope and the promise of restoration for any situation. Let *My Breaking Point, God's Turning Point* begin the healing of your heart and brighten your expectations for the future.

Donald Driver
Author, *New York Times* Bestseller, *Driven*
Super Bowl Champion, Green Bay Packers
Dancing with the Stars Winner, Season 14

Some can inspire, some possess eloquence, and some can write compellingly, but only a rare few are blessed with all three. My dear friend Pastor Ricky Texada is such a man, and this searingly honest book will transform and uplift every reader. With his wife, Cyd, a vital part of this valuable volume, Pastor Ricky provides powerful inspiration and compelling guidance. We all need it in our libraries.

Rabbi Daniel Lapin
American Alliance of Jews & Christians

There are some people who write books because they have something to say. Then there are people, like Ricky Texada, who write books because their life is a transformational example that others can benefit from. Within the pages of this book are more than just principles you can live by, but words that will *transform* your life. Ricky is the real deal who will help you deal with your real—so that whatever you *go* through, if you will *grow* through it, you will create a *breakthrough*!

Keith Craft
Pastor, Elevate Life Church, Frisco, Texas

From the moment I opened this book I experienced the liberating presence of God as I laughed, cried and worshiped. No doubt many comforting answers will slip from heaven and accompany the reader through the painful and beautiful saga of Ricky Texada's journey—oh, for grace to trust Him more.

Brett Jones
Pastor, Grace Church, Humble, Texas

This book is a gem: powerful, impacting and inspirational. Ricky Texada shares his compelling story that is certain to bring healing to all who join the journey. *My Breaking Point, God's Turning Point* will strengthen your faith in a loving, faithful and powerful God. You will be forever changed!

Frank King, J.D.
Pastor, Refreshing Waters Worship Center, Kansas City, Missouri

My Breaking Point, God's Turning Point is all about hope and the fulfillment of Jeremiah 29:11: "I know what I'm doing. I have it all planned out—plans to take care of you, not abandon you, plans to give you the future you hope for" (*THE MESSAGE*). The image we have of ourselves and our future is not always what God has planned. Pastor Ricky and Cyd are very real and transparent in telling their story of tragedy to triumph. They show us the importance of trusting in God when it does not seem practical or realistic. It is a book about finding the strength to get up one more time than you fall and knowing you will make it.

Darryl Carnley
Senior Pastor, Celebrate Life Church, Nampa, Idaho
Founding Pastor, North Pole Worship Center, North Pole, Alaska

Readers who are yearning to reestablish trust, understanding and compassion after devastating loss will embrace *My Breaking Point, God's Turning Point*. As Ricky Texada takes us to the heart of God's restorative and redemptive love for us, we are given insight into God's ability to turn even the darkest days into light. As he painstakingly reveals his journey from tremendous loss to a life beyond measure, Ricky shows us that God is faithful: God speaks to us about our responsibility in our relationship to Him, about His abiding promise of provision through His relationship to us as well as the relationships He puts in place for us. I highly recommend this life-changing, feel-good, brilliant book to those in need of a mental, physical and spiritual comeback!

Cyndi Miller, CEO
The Miller Companies, Dallas, Texas

MY
Breaking Point

GOD'S
Turning Point

EXPERIENCE GOD'S AMAZING
POWER TO RESTORE

RICKY TEXADA

BETHANYHOUSE
a division of Baker Publishing Group
www.BethanyHouse.com

Published by Bethany House Publishers
11400 Hampshire Avenue South
Bloomington, Minnesota 55438
www.bethanyhouse.com

Bethany House Publishers is a division of
Baker Publishing Group, Grand Rapids, Michigan
www.bakerpublishinggroup.com

Printed in the United States of America

Library of Congress Cataloging-in-Publication Data is on file at the Library of Congress, Washington, DC.

All Scripture quotations, unless otherwise indicated, are taken from the *Holy Bible, New International Version®. NIV®* Copyright © 1973, 1978, 1984, 2011 by Biblica, Inc.™ Used by permission of Zondervan. All rights reserved worldwide. www.zondervan.com The "NIV" and "New International Version" are trademarks registered in the United States Patents and Trademark Office by Biblica, Inc.™

Other versions used are
ESV—Scripture taken from the *English Standard Version,* Copyright © 2001. The *ESV* and *English Standard Version* are trademarks of Good News Publishers.
KJV—*King James Version.* Authorized King James Version.
THE MESSAGE—Scripture taken from *THE MESSAGE.* Copyright © by Eugene H. Peterson 1993, 1994, 1995, 1996, 2000, 2001, 2002. Used by permission of NavPress Publishing Group.
NKJV—Scripture taken from the *New King James Version.* Copyright © 1979, 1980, 1982 by Thomas Nelson, Inc. Used by permission. All rights reserved.
NLT—Scripture quotations marked *NLT* are taken from the *Holy Bible, New Living Translation,* copyright © 1996, 2004, 2007 by Tyndale House Foundation. Used by permission of Tyndale House Publishers, Inc., Carol Stream, Illinois 60188. All rights reserved.

Published in association with the literary agency of Dupree/Miller & Associates, Dallas, TX 75205.

14 15 16 17 18 19 20 | 7 6 5 4 3 2 1

In keeping with biblical principles of creation stewardship, Baker Publishing Group advocates the responsible use of our natural resources. As a member of the Green Press Initiative, our company uses recycled paper when possible. The text paper of this book is composed in part of post-consumer waste.

*This book is dedicated to my Lord and Savior Jesus Christ.
Because of Your love and commitment, I'm a free man. The story I tell is
not my own but Yours. You have allowed me to be a part of it.*

*To my sons, Seth and Caleb, you are the "Appointed" and
"Faithful" kings, respectively. When I look at you, I'm reminded that God
has an appointed time and place for everything and He is faithful forever.
The times we share, making up songs and our bedtime conversations
are invaluable. You both are destined for greatness!*

Contents

Do you want to get well? If we truly desire healing from our heart's pain, then we must go through the process of allowing God to work in our lives. We have to be wholehearted in our desire for God's restoration.

No matter how good our lives may look or how bad we may feel, we are not alone in our pain. We have all suffered and need to experience God's healing power and the restoration of our souls.

If we want to trust God with our deepest wounds, we must start where we are, acknowledging our feelings and taking the next small step as we move through our losses. In order to move through our pain, we must let go of our own expectations and reach out to accept what God wants to give us.

In order to experience God's redemptive love and transforming power in our lives, we must acknowledge the extent of our losses. Acknowledging what we've lost—all the "might have beens"—allows us to move through the pain of our loss instead of getting lost in the midst of it. When we cry out to God, He hears us and comforts us.

If we want to experience God's gifts, then we must listen to His voice and follow His guidance. Maintaining and restoring our trust in God requires us to accept His provision and to embrace the opportunities He sends our way. We must exercise faith and build trust by believing that God is truly for us, even when we don't understand our life's losses. When we know that He is for us, then we can experience peace, even in life's storms.

emotions. We must persevere through our trials and the restoration process and be grateful for the many traveling mercies along the way.

When we've suffered major loss in our lives, it's tempting to isolate ourselves through self-pity, detachment, anger and resentment. But the key to seeing God move in our lives often arrives through our relationships with other people as we serve and give of ourselves to address their needs. In fact, we help ourselves through our pain the most when we serve other people.

The Lord loves us, and His plans for us are for good. Even when others may intend to harm us, such as we see in the biblical story of Joseph, God uses hurtful events for our good. With a loving Father leading us, we can experience freedom to hope, joy to live with purpose, and peace to overcome the pain of the past—the fruits of restoration.

Foreword

I was honored to be asked to write the foreword for this book for several reasons. First, because of what I think of the author. Ricky Texada is one of the most outstanding men that I know—a man of principle, loyalty, character and kindness. Secondly, I know the story that he tells is true, touching and will be life-changing for the reader. Finally, I know that Ricky's greatest desire is to encourage you in your struggles in life by telling the story of God's faithfulness to him in his.

This is an amazing story that begins with a young man from the bayous of Louisiana who married his college sweetheart and headed to Dallas to begin his career and build a life. That was when I first met Ricky. He began attending our young church and eventually served in youth ministry under the watchful eye of my wife, Kathy.

Ricky was living a happy, successful life and planned to continue reaching for his career goals and looked forward to starting a family. Then life dealt him a sudden and tragic blow that changed his vision of his destiny in a moment, and set before him the most difficult choices a man could possibly have to make. I have watched Ricky walk out God's plan for his life—including the dark times—to emerge into the light of victory and fulfillment. His story will inspire you to accomplish all that God has planned for your life.

I am sure that, as you read this book, you will experience the same things that I did: hope, encouragement and determination to push through anything that is designed to slow our progress toward the ultimate joy of understanding that God is in control, and the plans He has for us are good! As you read this powerful book, prepare to be moved, challenged and ultimately uplifted.

Mike Hayes
Founding Pastor, Covenant Church and
Churches in Covenant International

Introduction

A Question of Healing

Restoration requires you to release your resistance to change.

Restoration begins the moment you stop defining yourself by your pain. It begins when you accept that you can't keep going as you have been and instead you allow God to give you the power to move on. It begins when you ask Him to give you a new perspective, a larger, timeless glimpse of how your breaking point can become a turning point.

Now before you stop reading and dismiss what I have to say as just another version of "let go and let God," I want to ask you a question that Jesus asked someone before He healed him. In this story of an ailing man, notice Christ's response, in the form of a question, to the man's suffering before He restored him:

> Now there is in Jerusalem near the Sheep Gate a pool, which in Aramaic is called Bethesda and which is surrounded by five covered colonnades. Here a great number of disabled people used to lie—the blind, the lame, the paralyzed. One who was there had been an invalid for thirty-eight years.
>
> When Jesus saw him lying there and learned that he had been in this condition for a long time, he asked him, *"Do you want to get well?"*
>
> "Sir," the invalid replied, "I have no one to help me into the pool when the water is stirred. While I am trying to get in, someone else goes down ahead of me."
>
> Then Jesus said to him, "Get up! Pick up your mat and walk." At once the man was cured; he picked up his mat and walked (John 5:2-9, emphasis added).

I don't know about you, but if I had been that lame man, an invalid for 38 years, and had been laying near this pool known for its healing properties, I might have been a little upset, even insulted, by Jesus' question. "Really? You're asking me if I want to get well? As I lie here, unable to stand or walk, barely able to crawl, You're curious to know if I want to get well?"

But we know that Jesus' question was not a cruel or insensitive one; the Master clearly had a sincere and caring reason for posing such a query to this man. I suspect His question has something to do with the Lord's understanding of human nature. Jesus knew that the lame man could not be healed unless he was willing to move beyond the suffering that had defined him for the past four decades.

His question resonates in our hearts today: "Do you want to get well? Do you want to be healed and restored? Are you willing to allow God to transform what feels like your breaking point into a portal of hopeful restoration?" If we truly desire healing from our heart's pain, then we must go through the process of allowing God to work in our lives. We have to be wholehearted in our desire for God's restoration.

Like the lame man, we need more than just one kind of healing. This man was likely focused on his physical limitations and sufferings, but Jesus addressed all areas of the crippled man's life with His question about getting well. Christ knows that when we suffer a major loss or disappointment in life, it affects our entire being—spirit, soul and body. And He also knows that if we are to heal and to experience the strength, hope and purpose that come from God's restoration process, then our healing must also be comprehensive.

As I reveal my bittersweet story with you in the pages that follow, I hope you will see that I share this with you because I believe that God's loving power is the only way to keep going in the midst of life's trials and tragedies. My loss threatened to consume me when it occurred, but God intervened in my situation in ways that I couldn't ignore. Although I wasn't waiting beside a pool to be healed, I might as well have been asked the same question that Jesus asked the lame man. I knew that I had a choice to make about how to face the devastating loss that forever altered my life.

I could choose to get well. Or I could choose to remain paralyzed by the crushing weight of my grief, pain and sorrow.

And that choice would have to be made daily—sometimes hourly—through those darkest days as God began restoring my strength, hope and confidence in His sovereignty.

You face the same choice. If you're reading these words, there's a good chance that your heart longs to experience the healing touch of God's hand. As scary as it may seem, admit the truth about how much you long to be restored, about how desperately you want to believe that God can surprise you.

Because He can if you'll let Him. He has a new life waiting for you. It's your choice, my friend.

Do you want to get well?

Then turn the page!

1

Step Out in Faith: Seeing More Than Meets the Eye

If you were to follow my family around with a camera as if we were part of some reality TV show, you might wonder what I know about suffering. My wife, Cyd, and I have two sons—one teenager, Seth, and one preteen, Caleb—and we live in a comfortable home in a nice neighborhood outside Dallas. Cyd and I serve together as pastors in the ministry of our vibrant, fast-growing church. We've been married over 15 years and still enjoy the passionate spark of connection that kindled our love in the first place.

Most days Cyd and I get started early with some personal time of prayer and reflection before we wake the boys and get the day going. Then the hours fly by in a flurry of getting the boys to school, working at the church, heading to sports and extracurriculars and arriving home for dinner, homework and whatever else we might need to do. Our tasks at work include Cyd coordinating a myriad of ministry details. I'm the visionary, manager and big-picture person; Cyd makes sure the details of vision implementation are identified so that our staff can carry them out.

Sound familiar? Regardless of the season we're in, most of us know how quickly each day seems to become a blur, spilling into the next day's demands and activities. It's easy for us to get caught up in the cycle of super busyness that pervades our culture.

Because of the demands placed on Cyd and me in ministry, our home is our refuge. Amidst the many books, Legos and Nerf gear, it's the place where we retreat after a busy day of ministry. Each evening as the boys prepare to go to bed, we share a Scripture reading and a discussion of the day's events together.

While our relationship with the Lord is preeminent, Cyd and I have consciously decided that ministry will never take precedence over family. We do our best not to openly discuss the issues or problems of people that we have encountered during the day in front of the boys. Ministry can be very challenging, but we want our boys to always have a positive view of ministry work.

Cyd is responsible for most of our meal preparation, home organization and homework (when school is in session). I'm responsible for coordinating family entertainment, which includes chasing the boys around the house, playing pool, dominating on Xbox (Seth might challenge that) and enjoying the mother of all fun—Nerf wars! Cyd makes sure that board games and movie nights and plenty of popcorn are also incorporated into the fun.

In our home we've tried our best to create an atmosphere in which the Lord is honored above all. As a result, our house is filled with lots of conversation and singing. My sons and I have been known to break into impromptu, lyrics-on-the-spot songs about anything and everything from the glories of the Lord to the joys of our favorite breakfast cereal. We usually keep going until we can't sing for laughing or until we start getting on Cyd's "last nerve."

Since Sundays are especially busy days, Cyd and I enjoy Monday as our day off and usually have lunch out together or go on some kind of date. And in our busy household, it's definitely important for us to have time alone. Whenever Cyd and I show any affection toward one another in front of the boys, they roll their eyes and act as if they don't like it, and they try to separate us. I'll push back and say, "Hey, she's my girlfriend! Mine, all mine!" They giggle uncontrollably, but I think they enjoy the shoving match that ensues as they try to push me away while I'm stealing a kiss from their mother.

Swimming in the Dark

While I know that my family is incredibly blessed, please don't think that we're perfect by any means. We're like any typical family that has disagreements, disputes, discussions and discipline, but our goal is to always resolve conflict as quickly as possible and not hold grudges. We encounter most of the same frustrations and obstacles that everyone faces—demands pulling us in too many directions, chores around the house never getting caught up, and bills that seem to multiply from month to month.

But as I said, if you followed me around on a typical day, I could understand why you might question my credibility to write this book. As my story unfolds, however, I believe that you'll agree that the joyful normalcy my family experiences now is only authentic because it was born out of the devastation that first brought Cyd and me together. In fact, I'm convinced that the main reason my life fulfills me so much now is that I was forced to endure a loss that I never could have imagined surviving.

I think that this process of suffering and surviving unimaginable losses binds us all together. People say that no matter how happy someone else appears to us, we can never know the burdens that the person is bearing. Besides my own experience, my pastoral involvement with thousands of hurting men and women confirms this. Many people work hard to appear successful, happy and fulfilled, while inside they don't know how they will make it through the next hour, let alone the rest of the day.

If you want to experience healing and restoration from the losses in your life, I can offer you great hope. However, the only way to reach the shores of healing is to swim through the murky depths between the place you are now and the place you want to be. It won't be easy, but the process of moving from grief to grace will surprise you and reactivate feelings, dreams and hopes that you thought had been extinguished forever. Like swimming in the ocean at night, it will require faith.

Show Your Stripes

Most of us don't like swimming when we can't see where we're going. Similarly, we don't know how to integrate loss into our lives.

Our culture has forgotten how to grieve and, consequently, how to heal. We seem to either run away from our painful losses or else get stuck in the midst of them. In the movies, on TV, in our songs and in our books, characters seem to find happy endings in neat story arcs and 30-minute segments. Perhaps it's not surprising then that the number of prescriptions for antidepressants and anti-anxiety drugs has more than quadrupled in the past decade.

Today there's more pressure than ever for people to be successful, to have their lives together, and to be headed in a direction that's always higher and better. We can earn degrees online, hire a personal life coach, attend money-management seminars, read the latest self-help book from a motivational guru, cultivate our love life with online dating, and make friends with just one click on a social-media site. Since there are so many ways to better ourselves in all these areas of our life, why would we settle for less?

Even as our society becomes virtually global and our culture diversely multi-ethnic, we still feel the urge to conform to some ideal of excellence. We've all heard that we have to put our best foot forward, look the part if we want to get the job, dress for success or even "fake it till we make it." With technology we can spin our success in countless ways, impressing everyone around us with not just who we are but also who we're becoming. In fact, I recently heard a friend refer to Facebook as Fakebook, because he's noticed that everyone seems to provide only great pictures of themselves in luxurious settings and change status only to indicate the next successful person they've met.

My friend doesn't feel as if there's room to be, well, human on such sites. Looking at a photo of a smiling, perfectly made-up face framed by a beautiful hairstyle is not the same as sitting across from someone and looking at the stories hiding in their eyes. There doesn't seem to be a lot of room these days for us to show our scars, our pain and the stripes we've earned from life's battles. But how we respond to our wounds will determine how we live our lives.

Chasing the Wind

At some point in our lives, most of us will experience a traumatic event that will change us forever, an encounter that will leave our body gasping for air and our soul grasping for meaning. For some people it may be dealing with the childhood betrayal of a parent or a trusted adult. Others may find this moment in an unplanned pregnancy, in the death of a spouse, in the loss of their job. It may be the jolt of a doctor's words delivering a frightening prognosis. It could be the ache of loneliness caused by divorce or the anguish of losing a home in a tornado, hurricane or wildfire. It could simply be waking up one day and realizing that a special opportunity has passed us by.

When faced with a powerful, unexpected loss, we naturally ask ourselves, "Why? What could I have done to deserve something so devastating?" We question God, crying out to Him, sometimes shaking our fist at Him, always asking for Him to take us out of our pain. We wonder why He didn't intervene and how such human suffering can be part of His divine plan.

As we lie in pain, writhing in whys and struggling to get back on our feet again, we wonder if it's worth it. Are we only getting back up just to be knocked over again down the road? During these times the words written in the Old Testament book of Ecclesiastes echo with new relevance: "All of it is meaningless, a chasing after the wind" (2:17). We can be walking through life one minute, enjoying the satisfaction of all our hard work paying off, and the next minute, the same dream that appeared to be just within reach suddenly slips through our fingers.

Any time we lose something in our lives, however, we also gain new perspective. I remain convinced that these crossroads of crisis always offer an individual choices: We can either lose hope completely and give up or we can gather the scattered remnants of our dreams, trusting that somehow God remains sovereign and has a plan for our lives—a plan that in the end will produce the intricate design of a beautifully woven tapestry, a magnificent mural of maturity that uses the fibers of pain to enhance the texture of our lives.

More to My Story

You may be saying, "I appreciate that you're a pastor and that you have to bring God into it, but you don't know what I've been through. You don't know what it feels like to have your entire life unravel into a knotted mess of broken threads. You don't understand how hard it is for me to get up in the morning and go through the motions of another day while I carry around this painful weight of loss inside me."

You're right. I don't know your specific losses. But I ask you to trust me until I share more about my own experiences, which I think will reinforce my credibility. And forgive me if this notion of trusting God in the midst of loss seems abstract and flowery, because to make it sound that way is not my intention at all. The world doesn't need another book that teaches us to deny our feelings and cover them with a veneer of Bible verses and religious jargon. We don't need more feel-good self-help books to tell us how we should handle our emotions.

My goal in writing this book is not to gloss over the wounds inflicted by life's traumas. Nor is it to revel in them, sinking into despair and refusing to fight the good fight. My hope, our hope—for my wife, Cyd, and I both want to share our joint story with you—is that you will learn to reframe the way you see your life's losses. My goal is that you would be challenged and inspired by what we've learned so that you will be able not only to get back on your feet but also to run the race of life with purpose, determination and joy. My prayer is that you would give God a chance to prove His faithfulness to you.

I don't have all the answers. And I don't claim to know why God allows suffering. But I do know that no matter how painful our circumstances may seem, God never abandons us. I know that no matter what happens to us, we still have choices as to how we will respond.

How do I know this?

Keep reading, my friend.

Just as in everyone's life, there's more to my story than meets the eye.

RESTORE AND RENEW

At the end of each chapter, I've included a few questions for you to consider as you embark on your journey of restoration. You might want to consider using a journal, either an electronic/virtual one online or the old-fashioned kind with pen and paper. Keeping your thoughts, feelings and responses together in one place will allow you to see how God is leading you to experience healing in your life over time. Even if you don't keep a journal, I encourage you to reflect on your responses to each question, allowing God to enter your pain and to heal your wounds.

1. What's the biggest challenge you're facing right now? What blocks your path toward God's restoration and renewal in your life?
2. How would someone meeting you for the first time today describe you? Would they be able to see your heartache and distress, or do you usually keep them hidden?
3. How would you describe your relationship with God presently? Do you pray each day? Do you spend time in Bible study or meditation on Scripture? Are you part of a church or community of believers?
4. Do you trust God right now? If you could ask Him any question about what you've suffered in life, what would you ask?
5. How would you answer Jesus' question to the lame man: "Do you want to get well?"

RECONNECT AND REVIVE

After you've considered your responses, conclude your thoughts and reflections on each chapter by sharing them with God in prayer. Toward that goal of reconnecting with the One who remains committed to your heart's resurrection, I will provide a sentence or two to help you get started. There's no magic formula or "right way" that you must pray. The key is simply to open up the lines of heartfelt communication between you and your Father. Be honest, be real, and be open to what God has for you as He begins the process of restoration in your life.

Dear God, my heart is sore, and I'm so very tired. You know better than anyone the burdens I carry. I'm struggling to get back on my feet, Lord, and I need Your help. I surrender to You and ask You to come into my life and begin the process of restoration that only You can carry out. Amen.

2

Make a Date: Discovering the Next Chapter of Your Destiny

It was the summer of 1976. Al Wilson's "I've Got a Feeling that We'll Be Seeing Each Other Again" was on the radio, and I found myself singing the song over and over—especially after meeting a beautiful young lady named Stacey. She was 11, like me, and she had silky brown skin, long dark hair that flowed smoothly down her back and the biggest brown eyes I had ever seen, not to mention the cutest smile. She lived in Houston and had come to "the bayou," where I lived, to spend the summer with her grandparents. My preadolescent mind (fueled by an early infusion of hormones, no doubt) thought that we were a match made in heaven.

Our passionate relationship began with a series of phone calls. At first we had very interesting conversations on the phone every day, keeping things casual since I was too young to drive the five miles to her grandparents' house and too afraid to ride my bicycle that far. So ours had to begin as a short long-distance relationship. Those meaningful conversations included the intimate details of tree climbing, frog chasing, baseball tossing and TV watching with lots of silent, heavy breathing in between. You can tell what a silver-tongued Casanova I was, can't you?

Our conversations continued like this for several weeks until the middle of July. Then a party was held in the neighborhood where Stacey's grandparents lived. I only had to ask my dad once if I could go to the party. The look on his face told me everything I needed to know about whether an 11-year-old kid should attend a party with kids five, six or seven years older than he was. In fact, it was only because Stacey was being chaperoned by her teenage aunts that she was allowed to attend. So even though I couldn't go, my oldest brother, Greg, and our cousin, Charles, planned to be there and to serve as my spies.

I could hardly wait until Greg arrived home that evening so I could hear all the details of what happened at the party: Who was there? How many people attended? Was there drinking? How about any fights? And most of all, what did Stacey look like? Who was she talking to? Were any other boys hanging around her?

As I gazed intently at him, the recon Greg brought back was not what I had expected. He cut to the chase and informed me that he had seen Stacey kissing a boy at the party. Time stopped, and my heart screamed, "NOOOOOOOOOO!" As my brother shared this with me, he displayed no sensitivity (as if 15-year-old boys even know the meaning of the word). He simply delivered the news and began laughing and teasing me that my girl was playing the field on me. I couldn't believe my ears and would not believe Greg until my cousin Charles confirmed the same.

How could she do this to me? Didn't she know that I would give the world to her even though I didn't have two nickels to rub together? Didn't she have some sense of honor, decency and dignity? What kind of girl was she? I was completely devastated and utterly humiliated. In spite of all I felt, I had to do what a man had to do.

The next day I picked up the phone and called Stacey. I confirmed the facts with her that she had indeed gone to the party and had kissed a 15-year-old boy named Ronnie. I expressed my heart to her and the betrayal I felt. I told her that we were through. Whether she extended an apology or not, I don't remember. The only sound I could hear was the pounding of my own broken heart. Needless to say, my new favorite song became "Let's Just Kiss and Say Goodbye," sung by The Manhattans.

Leap of Faith

Now I realize that this devastating loss may still leave room for doubt regarding my credibility to discuss suffering. And while anyone might think this, I still learned a very important lesson from Stacey—a lesson about expectations. This truth was confirmed for me through other more serious losses as well as by hundreds of conversations I've had with other people. For most of us, the hardest part of moving through any significant life loss is adjusting our expectations.

We were just living our life, heading in a certain direction, imagining a particular kind of future with specific people, when suddenly the story we were scripting fell apart. Something happened—something we'd probably never imagined—and forever changed the fabric of our destiny. Or did it?

Surely if God is all-knowing and all-powerful, and I believe that He is, then He must have known that a curveball was coming our way. We can never see what's just around the next corner, but God always knows. And, as we'll explore together, this is where we have to make an important choice. Will we let go of the story we had planned on living out and allow ourselves to be caught up in the story that our Creator wants to tell? Or will we keep trying to change the past, reading and rereading the same page instead of beginning the next chapter?

Making the leap from what we expected to what feels like complete uncertainty requires an enormous risk of faith. And it begins with those first steps—baby steps. When we are forced to realize that our life will not unfold according to our own vision, then we must get used to walking in the dark.

When Cyd and I first moved into our present home, I would sometimes wake up during the night and get up for a drink of water or to use the bathroom. In a new place, with the bed and other furniture in an unfamiliar arrangement, I would usually bump into the corner of something. It was painful, and I didn't like it, but I didn't let that keep me from living in our new house. We may not like walking in the dark, but when we take that first step, we often discover that God will illuminate our path, one step at a time.

Lost Without Your Love

I know this firsthand because even asking Cyd out on a date was an enormous step for me. It's not that I was shy or that I lacked self-confidence to approach this beautiful woman. It had much more to do with the devastating loss I'd experienced prior to our first date—one that cut much deeper than what might have been with my old pal Stacey. More about this in a moment.

For now let me just say that dating was not a priority in my life. In fact, I was in the midst of an incredibly powerful time of prayer and fasting in which God had revealed to me a glimpse of the future to which He was calling me. This message was reinforced by our senior pastor during a prayer time I'd been part of at the church in which I was serving.

As I walked to my car after the church service that day, a tall guy named Keith Craft jumped out of Pastor Mike Hayes's truck and came running toward me, arms wildly flailing. Keith was a homeboy from Louisiana who stood around six feet six and weighed about 260 pounds. He had the body of a great college athlete.

As a body builder, he had remained in excellent shape since college and had a personality and a heart as big as Texas. Keith was a traveling evangelist and a motivational speaker. Little did I know that the conversation he and I would have that day would be the beginning of a new chapter in my divine destiny.

Keith approached me with his eyes open wide, the biggest, silliest grin on his face and a CD in his hand. He grabbed me by the shoulders and growled, "Brother! Do you know a girl named Cyd Patton?" and he showed me her picture on the CD cover. As I glanced at her new release, "I'm Lost Without Your Love," I thought, *Wow, she's more beautiful than I remembered.*

I said, "Yes, I know who she is. But I don't really know her. We went to college together." I recalled that Cyd had represented her class as Miss Freshman while I had served as sophomore class president in the student government. I remembered that she always seemed to have the biggest smile on her face whenever I saw her.

And she had a beautiful voice. I even discussed my view of the Christian faith with her in an attempt to get her on board with a more disciplined approach.

As with many young adults, in college I had plenty of passion for the Lord but no commonsense wisdom. I'd thought back then that if someone wasn't up at five in the morning interceding in prayer for at least an hour, he or she couldn't claim to be a real Christian. Cyd did not have a bad reputation; she just wasn't as rigorously focused on her faith as I was at the time.

Suddenly, as I stood next to my car as Keith and I were speaking, a memory flashed through my mind. I had entered the student government offices, and Cyd had been playing the piano and singing the most touching song: "You Gave Me Love" by B. J. Thomas. I could still hear her sweet, melodic voice: "You gave me laughter after I cried all my tears. You heard my dreams, while the rest of the world closed its ears. You smiled at me, while there were just frowns everywhere. You gave me love when nobody gave me a prayer. That's why I call You Savior. That's why I call You Friend. You touched my heart, You touched my soul, and helped me start all over again . . ."

When I'd heard Cyd singing that song, I had wondered how she could sing a song like that and not be serious about her walk with the Lord. Or maybe she had been serious but had just chosen not to wear her faith on her sleeve the way I had, for I later found out that she eventually became a praise singer for Bethany World Prayer Center. And now, almost a decade later, to hear about her again . . .

Keith explained to me that, the prior Sunday, he had ministered at Cyd's church in Arlington, Texas, about an hour from where our church was located. As a matter of fact, he had ministered there many times throughout the years and had gotten to know Cyd because of her incredible voice and bright smile. The previous weekend she had approached him and asked if he attended Covenant Church. When Keith had told her that he did, Cyd asked him if he knew a Ricky Texada, an acquaintance of hers from college.

Keith replied that he knew me well and would pass along Cyd's greeting to me. She had apparently heard that I was going through a tough season in my life and wondered if I was okay. However, when Keith shared with me that he'd told Cyd I would call her,

I wasn't excited about that at all. In fact, I was a little upset. The last thing on my mind was dating, finding a girlfriend or looking for a wife.

It had been a long time since I had even had a friendly phone conversation with a woman. I was currently on a spiritual fast that I didn't know how long would last. I was more focused on God than I had ever been up to that time. My relationship with Him was so intimate and special that I didn't want anyone interfering with it.

Seeing himself as a divinely inspired matchmaker, Keith sensed my uncertainty and added, "You'll call her, right? You're not going to make me into a liar, are you?" With that I gave in and asked him for Cyd's phone number. With a look of shock and disappointment, Keith realized that he'd failed to get her telephone number. We got a big laugh out of that, and I teased him, "What kind of matchmaker are you? I'll have to call directory assistance to get her number!"

In my office later that afternoon, I tracked down Cyd's number and jotted it on a sticky note, but I didn't dial it for another two months.

Call Me, Maybe

The reason I didn't call was twofold. First, I didn't want anything or anyone to interfere with my spiritual fast, which ended up lasting 40 days. I grew closer to the Lord than ever before and felt His presence and His transforming power in my life. And second, because I wanted to depend on God and had heard Him speak into my loneliness, I didn't want to be distracted by the prospect of a relationship. I didn't want to call Cyd just to avoid being alone with myself and alone with God. I had determined that I wouldn't entertain even a phone conversation unless I was completely whole emotionally.

So a couple months later, I walked into my office at the church after completing a meeting. As I sat down at my desk and looked at the telephone number on the small yellow sticky note that had been sitting there for the past two months. My stomach was in knots as I dialed the number and the phone began to ring. Thoughts were racing through my mind about what I would say; I felt like a teenage boy again instead of a grown man. As I listened to the phone ringing, I realized that it had been over 15 years since I'd called a woman for no other reason than a friendly chat. I resolved that I would make the conversation succinct, keep my word given to Keith Craft and move on with my life.

Cyd picked up. "Hello."

My mouth went dry. "Hi, may I speak to Cyd? This is Ricky Texada—I spoke to Keith Craft a couple of months ago and promised him I would call you."

"Yes, it's great to hear from you—I was wondering if you might call." We chatted for a few awkward moments, and I joked that at least now Keith would be off my back about connecting with her. Cyd explained that she was usually at choir rehearsal on Tuesday evenings, rain, shine, sleet or hail, but for the first time that she could remember, choir rehearsal had been canceled that night because of icy conditions. "I'm glad you called," she told me.

As we visited, we caught up on what had happened in each other's lives since college. She listened to my questions about her life and her work and told me that she was a systems design engineer who integrated smart weapons onto F-16 fighter jets and provided training for Air Force fighter pilots on the use of these weapons systems.

She mentioned how the church she attended had gone through a transitional season after the founding pastor had retired. Some of the leadership had left to start their own churches, and many of her friends as well had left to attend these new churches. Some had tried to coax her into joining them and wondered why she wouldn't budge. Her response had been, "God hasn't told me to go anywhere else. The last thing I remember Him telling me was to come to this church, and I haven't heard anything different." Cyd understood that her commitment was first to God and that He was the One who, many years before, had directed her to where she was.

She also shared with me how her male friends at work always chided her about becoming an old maid, saying that all she did was go to work and church. How could she ever find a husband doing that? But she informed them that she didn't have to go looking for a husband, because if God wanted her to be married, He would bring the man to her.

I couldn't believe my ears! I could tell by the quiet confidence in her voice that Cyd wasn't just saying this to create a "hard to get" dynamic. She was clearly not in any hurry to get ahead of whatever—or whomever—God had for her. Our conversation was so refreshing!

You Talking to Me?

It's often difficult to discern the voice of God amidst the noise and clamor of our busy lives, let alone when we're hurting or grieving. We want to hear the Lord and follow His guidance, to discern the whisper of His Spirit in our hearts, but it's difficult to do that when we can't hear ourselves think. Painful emotions can numb us and make us hard of hearing.

While modern technology may have compounded this issue, the problem is not a new one. I think of people like Moses, who encountered God in the burning bush (see Exod 3:1-2:17), Gideon, who experienced His presence under an oak tree as he threshed wheat (see Judg. 6:11-12), or Jonah, who floundered in the belly of a whale (see Jon. 2:1-10). Or especially the young Samuel, who woke up in the night and heard a voice three times before realizing who it was and telling the Lord, "Speak, for your servant is listening" (1 Sam. 3:10).

In each case and in numerous others, people question what they are hearing and being instructed to do. Moses didn't think that he was qualified to lead the children of Israel out of Egypt against Pharaoh's tight grip on them. He told God that he was not a good speaker and begged the Lord to choose someone else. God made it clear to Moses that he was His man, and then He used him for the most dramatic Exodus imaginable.

Gideon, bless his heart, was so caught off guard by the angel of the Lord addressing him as mighty warrior that he thought there had been a mistake. Can't you just imagine him looking over his shoulder and wondering who God was talking to? But after a lengthy exchange—and a few fleeces—God again made His message and His plan for Gideon crystal clear.

And with Jonah we're also reminded that it's impossible to run away from God, no matter how hard we may try to do so. We can choose to ignore His message or disobey Him, but God doesn't give up on us. He understands the fear, doubt, anger and pain with which His human children struggle. All the more reason that He keeps speaking into our lives and encouraging us to take heart and to act on faith. God never abandons us, even when the brunt of life's storms leaves us bullied and bruised.

The choice is ours, however. And from my experience, the decision ultimately comes down to how we answer only one question: *Do we believe that God is for us, despite the painful evidence surrounding us?* It's not an easy question to ask, let alone answer, and we'll explore it throughout the rest of the pages of this book. For now I would simply ask you to reflect on how you hear God in your life presently and how you've been responding to Him.

The Dating Game

Despite my reluctance to call Cyd and possibly launch a new relationship with her, I sensed that God was up to something in my reconnection with her. For one thing, that initial phone conversation lasted almost three hours! Cyd was easy for me to talk with and seemed so witty and compassionate. By the end of our conversation, as we were both amazed at how much time had passed, I knew what I needed to do and what God wanted me to do: I needed to ask Cyd out on a date. But it still felt incredibly scary to take the risk and put myself out there.

And I wasn't sure which would be worse: for Cyd to say yes or for her to say no! If she agreed to go, that would mean that the door of my heart would only open more, possibly allowing her into my life, a scary proposition indeed. If she said no, I would be confused and would question why she and I had reconnected after all these years, not to mention that I'd feel the sting of rejection.

My heart was racing a thousand beats per minute when I finally mustered the nerve to ask Cyd to dinner. This was monumental for me, since I had not been on a first date with any woman in over 16 years. What did I know about dating? How had courting changed over the years? It felt very strange yet exhilarating as I asked her, "Would you like to have dinner on Saturday evening?"

"Let me check my calendar," Cyd replied, which she later confirmed to me had been a ploy to keep her from saying yes too quickly. Finally, however, after replying to my question with an affirmative response, Cyd recommended a place that had great crawfish etouffee: Mac's Bar & Grill just off Green Oaks Boulevard in Arlington. I asked if I should pick her up at her place, but she declined and suggested meeting at the restaurant. *A wise woman*, I thought to myself. I later learned the real reason that she hadn't wanted me to pick her up: She'd thought that if I was boring, she didn't want to have all that time with me in such a confined space, since the restaurant was about a half-hour drive from her place.

I could hardly wait to talk with Cyd again the next day, although I didn't want her to know how anxious I was to speak with her. For the next three days, she and I talked by phone every night—with each visit learning new things about each other. It was wonderful conversing with someone with whom I felt safe. She was 60 miles away, she didn't attend Covenant Church (dating someone I served as a member of my congregation would have put me into an awkward role), and I could get to know her without any expectations.

Risky for a Reason

Sometimes I think that God wants us to take risks simply to remind us that we don't know everything. When we get those pesky expectations in mind, they're hard to shake. We start thinking that we know what someone else will say or what they'll do, maybe how they'll feel—or even what we ourselves will say or do or feel in certain situations. The reality, however, is that risk is just that—risky. Even if we are only taking small steps forward in our risks, we're still moving into an unknown future.

Lurking in that uncertainty could be something or someone who will pull the scab off our wounds or press into the bruises of our past battles. Worse, we may encounter new losses that we never saw coming—the loss of a child, the betrayal of our spouse, disappointment in our boss or the collapse of our finances, just to name a few.

But this is where faith comes in. For faith fuels our ability to take the next step, no matter how small that step may seem. We dare to hope that somehow doing the next thing that needs doing, taking the next stride toward our future, can somehow alleviate the pain and loneliness we're feeling. Maybe even more than that, we hope that taking the next step will somehow help us make sense of our loss.

While we may never understand our painful losses, our baby steps—making a date, in my case—can change us. Not because they enable us to move away from our losses but because they remind us that we're still capable of moving at all. When we take a small step forward, we realize that we're not as stuck as we thought.

Fear at First Sight

This was certainly the case as I anticipated my first date with Cyd. Saturday could not arrive soon enough. The tension in my emotional atmosphere as I went about my usual errands that day surrounded me like a fog. As I got dressed, I found myself being unusually fussy about my hair and clothes, neither of which I had paid much attention to for some time. That evening as I drove down the interstate, I worshiped the Lord with Hillsong, trying to preoccupy my mind and heart so that I wouldn't be so nervous.

I arrived at the restaurant a few minutes early in order to make a good impression, so I was disappointed that Cyd was not already there. I'm not the fretting kind, but I wondered if she had gotten cold feet or had forgotten about our dinner. I had to remind myself that I was there a little early. Sure enough, she arrived a couple minutes later, early herself.

As she walked toward me, the first thing I noticed was her huge smile and those beautiful lips covered with a shade of plum-colored lipstick. As I mentioned, she had been known around campus for her warm, dazzling smile, and it was still as stunning as ever. With her long brown hair falling below her shoulders and her smooth, cream-colored complexion radiating with life, Cyd commanded the attention of everyone in the room. She was simply beautiful.

As she continued in my direction, I stood to my feet and began to walk toward her, all the while noticing the light in her brown eyes that danced with such life. She extended her hand for a handshake, which I appreciated, since I didn't want to seem too familiar by giving her a hug. Plus, as a pastor representing my church as well as the

Lord, I always tried to show the utmost respect to others in all my public as well as private functions. Cyd, wearing a white blouse with ruffled collar and sleeves, a black skirt and tall black boots, looked stunning, and I told her as much when we were seated at the table.

Our conversation that evening covered the full gamut of our families, careers, travels, hopes and dreams. We spent time talking about her life as a professional single woman and why she had not married yet. Cyd was so transparent about her life and family as well as the struggles and temptations she faced as a single person. I also noticed how she wolfed down a lot of food, and I chuckled to myself, thinking that some things never change. Cyd had been known in college as the little lady who could eat more food than two grown men—all without gaining an ounce.

By the time the conversation had ended, we had eaten a salad, crawfish etouffee, gumbo, hushpuppies and Mac's famous gold-brick brownie sundae. More than three hours had seemed like only a few minutes, and I felt sad that our time together was over. As we made our way to the parking lot, I found out just how feisty she really was: Cyd drove a sporty royal blue Mazda Miata convertible! The car suited her and reminded me how much I loved her zeal for living, her passion for being alive to the fullest.

Before we parted company, Cyd and I gave each other a friendly hug. We agreed to check our schedules and determine the next available time for a dinner date.

As I walked back to my car, I said to the Lord, "Cyd is a lovely woman, and she seems to be someone I could pursue as my wife. If this is Your will, please reveal this to me very quickly." If God didn't show me within a couple of months, I had no intention of getting caught up in a long-term relationship. Cyd seemed like a wonderful lady, but I just didn't know if I could risk getting into a relationship with her. Or, really, with anyone.

You see, it wasn't my childhood crush on Stacey that had caused me to build the real walls around my heart. Early in my adult journey, I had found the love of my life, an amazing woman named Debra, and had married her. We had been happier than two people could be, serving in ministry together, planning our future together, imagining the family we would have.

And then I lost her.

RESTORE AND RENEW

1. Have you experienced a season in which it seemed like you were starting over? What did you learn about yourself during that time? About God?
2. What are you presently being called to risk as you move into a new season of restoration? How have you seen God's hand in this prompting?
3. List the top three fears that prevent you from taking a risk right now and stepping out in faith. After identifying them, I challenge you to find three different verses (one for each fear) that remind you of God's truth in the face of fear.
4. Where do you see yourself six months from now? One year? How will you get there? What's one step you can take today toward the future God has for you?

RECONNECT AND REVIVE

Lord, I know that You have gone before me and have prepared the way. But I still get scared, and I worry about being hurt and disappointed again. Give me Your courage to take the risk that You want me to take, trusting that You are with me each step of the way. Amen.

3

Share Your Burden: Respecting the Fullness of What You've Lost

Whenever I'm having a Nerf-gun battle with my sons—a shootout more intense than any Western movie or Xbox game can offer—or playing basketball or even doing homework, I'm reminded of one of my favorite things about kids: their imaginations. They have no trouble suspending their disbelief when they're watching superheroes soar through the air or in seeing themselves as Lebron on the court. Even the much-dreaded homework becomes fun for them if there's a way to turn it into something creative, whether that's devising a story about events in history or drawing a picture to illustrate the biological parts of a frog.

Yes, the human imagination is a wonderful thing and surely one of God's precious gifts to each of us. However, the same capacity that enables us to enjoy *The Hobbit* or paint a beautiful landscape also creates in us something that often hinders our ability to heal: expectations. When life is going a certain way, most people like to imagine that it will either continue in the same way (especially if things are going well) or become better than it is in our current circumstances. Even pessimists and chronic worriers—in other words, people who often imagine worst-case scenarios—don't want to experience loss and heartache.

We never expect to lose what we have, even if we know rationally that we won't be able to keep everyone and everything that we presently enjoy. The mortality of our bodies and the process of change over time remain parts of life that are permanently grounded in the world around us. Kids grow up. Relationships change. Houses require more maintenance. Workers retire. And people we love pass away. The Bible asks us to consider, "What is your life? You are a mist that appears for a little while and then vanishes" (Jas. 4:14).

Even though we know that loss is part of life, and even though we may find it natural to comfort others and be there for them when they're hurting, when rough things happen to us, it's never easy. Maybe part of the reason is that we have to adjust our expectations and try to imagine our lives without whatever or whomever we've lost. Often this seems impossible—we simply can't imagine living without that person or starting over somewhere else. We end up feeling blocked, stuck, stunned and leveled by what we didn't see coming.

At least that's the way I felt.

Like Any Other Day

December 17, 1996, began like any other day. I usually woke up earlier than my wife, Debra, who was a night owl and often worked late into the night. We both knew that she would oversleep if I didn't eventually wake her up. When we had begun dating in college, I realized that Debra had no consciousness of time. That morning was no different; I was up and eager to start the day while she slowly got going.

A half hour after I woke her up, as I sat on the edge of our bed, completely dressed and ready to go, Debra peered from the closet and asked me which pair of shoes she should wear. When I chose the tan patterned heels over the plain brown flats, she smiled and said, "I thought you would pick those."

We were both in a good mood and eager to get to the church where we were both on staff. The night before Debra had felt uneasy, and we had prayed together a long time before she had felt peaceful enough to relax and eventually drift off to sleep. But this morning seemed filled with the joy of a new day, one that makes a person grateful for all it has to unfold.

While we usually ate lunch together, that day Debra joined her close-knit group of girlfriends to celebrate someone's birthday. At the end of the day, she and I met in her office to plan for an evening meeting when our boss, Pastor Mike Hayes, popped in to share some good news with us. Fresh from a pastoral team meeting, he told us that the church leadership team had voted to ordain both Debra and me as pastors at the beginning of the New Year.

As I watched her eyes twinkling upon hearing Pastor Mike's exciting news, I remembered a private joke we shared. Whenever the topic of my calling to be a pastor came up, Debra always said, "When you become a pastor, I'm going to buy you some black wingtip shoes and a Cadillac!" We always laughed together at her promise that drew on the trademark possessions of preachers in the rural area of Louisiana where she'd grown up.

We went into our evening meeting in good spirits and achieved the outcome we'd hoped to attain. Debra, typically a quiet, behind-the-scenes kind of leader, had commented frequently, and I complimented her afterward on her insightful eloquence. As we wrapped up and prepared to head home, I said, "Isn't it exciting that we're going to be ordained? Who would have thought it! Growing up in the small town of Morrow, Louisiana, did you ever imagine that God would lead you to become a pastor?"

"No," she exclaimed, smiling. "But I've always known that I've found favor with Him!"

Blindsided

We continued our cloud-nine conversation on the drive home. Debra traced the path from our college days, when we were both struggling to pay for school, to our wedding day and the many trips we'd taken together since. She cited all the people we had allowed to stay with us rent-free while they got their financial footing. She listed all the ministries to which we had contributed our time, energy and resources.

"Ricky," she concluded, "we've been blessed to minister to more people in our 10 years of marriage than some people accomplish in a lifetime. We have had such an amazing life together!"

Nodding in agreement, I felt my stomach rumble, which reminded me of an invitation from a good friend of ours. Pat had invited us to stop by for some of her homemade gumbo, but I had forgotten to mention it to Debra until that moment.

"What do you think?" I asked, as we slowed for a stoplight. "Are you up for some good ol' spicy Cajun food?"

She thought for a moment and said, "I just want to go home," just as the traffic signal turned green and I prepared to turn left. Suddenly and unexpectedly, WHAM! Something careened into us, and the collision made a sound like a massive thunderclap. Time slowed and seemed to move like cold molasses as we floated forward and sharply came to a wild stop.

I don't know how much time passed before I swam back to consciousness. Probably only a few seconds, maybe a minute. "What happened?" Fighting my seatbelt, I turned to Debra in the passenger seat—only she wasn't there. Startled, I quickly glanced over my right shoulder and saw her sitting in the backseat, her head bowed as if in prayer.

"Debra? *Baby?* Debra!" I kept calling her name, realizing that she must be unconscious, when I noticed a dark, maroon stain growing across the front of her silk blouse. I had to get her out of there as quickly as possible. With a sudden surge of adrenaline, I unstrapped my mangled seatbelt and forced open my door. Jammed, it finally groaned open, and I pried myself out of the car.

At that moment, standing in the dimly lit street, I realized that we had been in an accident. The crumpled left fender and buckled frame of our white Olds 98 made it look like an extended accordion that someone had abandoned. I tried to remember what had happened—I had been making a left, turning west onto Rosemeade. Now the car rested about 50 feet from the intersection and faced east.

I hurriedly opened the back right passenger door, only to be stunned by the sight of blood gushing out of Debra's mouth. Her heart was still beating, so I began to pray, declaring, "This is not going to end like this!" No, no, absolutely not. I had glimpsed the future that the Lord had for me and my wife and for our ministry, and this scene was not part of it.

"Hang in there, baby—you're going to be okay," I said, placing my hand in the center of her back, torn between wanting to try to stop the blood flow and not wanting to exacerbate any internal injuries. I continued praying, "You will raise her up, because it is not supposed to end this way."

Noticing the crowd that had started to gather, I yelled out, "Phone! Anyone have a phone?" even as an approaching siren signaled the ambulance's arrival. Cell phones were so new. I didn't even have one yet, but I had just bought one for Debra and had planned on giving it to her for Christmas. Everything suddenly seemed to happen at once. If time had poured by me thick and slow only minutes ago, a flood of urgency now washed over me. Paramedics attended to Debra. More people gathered. A second ambulance and several police cars arrived.

With a stranger's phone still in hand, I dialed a number that I knew by heart, that of a youth pastor and dear friend from church, Gordon Banks. He immediately began to pray and promised to meet me at the hospital. Later he was at the hospital along with Pastor Mike and our operations pastor, Jeff Driver, and eventually dozens of others from our church.

We were rushed to the hospital's ER. It was not until we arrived at the hospital that I realized that the left side of my body was numb. There one of the law enforcement officers investigating the accident told me that a drunk driver had run through the red light and crashed into us going over 70 miles per hour in a 45 zone. As I was being examined, I learned from the physician who had performed Debra's CT scan that she had severe head trauma and that her brain was swelling.

Dazed, confused and shaken, I tried to focus on what had happened, all while praying repeatedly and desperately for the Lord to protect my wife and to save her from the severity of her injuries. *How could this have happened?* I kept thinking, desperately wanting to go and be with Debra but also aware of the intense pain creeping up the left side of my body.

Finally, the door opened and Pastor Mike entered my exam room. Our eyes met, and I sensed great compassion and tenderness from him mixed with pain and disbelief. Even before he told me, "She's gone," tears had started to trickle down my face as an enormous pit opened within my soul.

I learned that Pastor Mike and two other pastors had been with Debra as she peacefully slipped into eternity.

She was gone.

Unthinkable

Speechless. Even now words can't adequately convey the impact of that moment.

Only 33 years old. The woman with whom I had planned to grow old and build a family. For 15 years she had been the only woman I had loved. Now she was taken from me by the reckless hands of a drunk driver. *How could this be?*

My tears began to flow uncontrollably as my pastor moved closer to my hospital bed. Both my hands went high above my head as I surrendered my pain in worship to the Lord. An intensely heavy pain seared my entire body. Everything in me hurt, simply ached. At that moment I felt that no one could begin to understand the depth of my pain except my heavenly Father. As painful as losing Debra was in that moment, I knew that the safest place, the only place that could offer comfort, was in His arms.

Although I felt myself drowning in disbelief and sorrow, I made two declarations to the forces greater than me. My first one was directed to the enemy, the one who is committed to the utter destruction of humanity: "If you think this is going to make me turn my back on God, you're in for a surprise. Watch me! I'm going to serve Him with even greater fervency. You will not win!"

And to my God I prayed, "Lord, You are the superintendant of my life, and You have seen this day. For some reason You have chosen not to intervene." My final words echoed those of a man who had lost much more than I had—but what I'd lost felt like everything to me. "Lord, though You slay me, yet will I serve You!" This prayer resulted from my devotions in the book of Job earlier that year. Little had I known when reading about the struggles and heartache of this man that I would soon find myself facing such depth of anguish.

In that moment maybe I didn't care if I lived or died; it hurt so bad to think of my life without my wife that in a way I felt as if I had been slain. In a matter of moments, everything that mattered most to me had been taken from me. But my faith, no matter how unraveled my life seemed, remained intact. God was all I had left.

Small Mercies

Now before you think I'm some kind of special saint or super Christian, please understand that even in my grief I knew that I had to turn to God with the excruciating depths of my pain. I didn't have to think about things or consider withdrawing from God. As Peter explained, "Lord, to whom shall we go? You have the words of eternal life" (John 6:68).

Was I angry? Yes. Confused? Of course. And sad? With an intensity beyond anything I had ever felt in my life. But to deny that God exists, is sovereign and loves me would have been like refusing to breathe. God had worked in my life and seen me through enough trials and heartaches for me to know that He had not abandoned me. I had nowhere to turn with my pain but to my Father. With the kind of searing pain that was reverberating through my body, mind and soul, only He could begin to soothe and comfort me.

So often our impulse is to pull away from everyone—including God, or even especially God, in some cases—because our loss feels so overwhelming. We feel numb. Detached. The details of life seem unimportant, and the reality we once knew has become a surreal dream, a nightmare.

Perhaps it's the unexpected nature of certain losses that seem to compound our heartache. If God knows everything—which He does—and is all-powerful—which He is—then how could He allow these kinds of loss to occur without warning? If the truth be told, it probably wouldn't have been any easier if I had known that Debra was going to be taken from me that mild winter day so many years ago. But I tell myself that at least I would've been able to say goodbye, to begin the process of letting go before the soul-bond of marriage that we shared was so dramatically, savagely severed.

As strange as it might sound, though, I've wondered if perhaps the unexpectedness of certain losses might be one of the small mercies God grants us. Would knowing about that wreck and what it would cost Debra and me ahead of time have made a difference? Assuming that I couldn't have prevented it from happening,

I'm not sure that knowing in advance would have helped. It would have allowed me to focus those precious hours, days or weeks on my relationship with this woman I loved as my wife, but this may have only made it harder—instead of easier—to let go when the time came.

In fact, loss, by its definition, always means that something has been taken away. But most of us don't like to have anything taken away, especially people we love or items we cherish, whether tangible, like jewelry, or intangible, like our career. Some people don't even want difficult or hard things taken away, because at least there's comfort in their familiarity.

But loss requires us to exercise our faith in the most crucial way possible. In the midst of grief, our first impulse may be something other than to turn to God for comfort, and that's okay. It's never too late, though, for us to express our pain to Him and to allow Him to comfort us. This requires letting go and acknowledging all the scary emotions that envelop us—fear, anger, sorrow, confusion and regret. While many people view a loss as God testing our faith, I wonder if in our losses perhaps He's simply allowing us to mature in our faith.

Baby Steps

When a baby finds her legs and begins to stand and then to toddle and walk, she inevitably falls down. There's no way around it. The only alternative would be to carry her and never allow her to stand on her own two feet and walk and eventually run. Obviously, carrying a child or a teenager or an adult sounds silly, and no parent wants to do it. We want our children to mature and to walk for themselves.

In the same way, what if God allows us to be leveled by grief so that we can get back on our feet and discover our strength in Him?

What if there's no other way for us to grow closer to God and to depend on Him as deeply as we want to? What if there's no other way for us to know ourselves and what we believe?

As author, scholar and theologian C. S. Lewis explains in *A Grief Observed*, "You never know how much you really believe anything until its truth or falsehood becomes a matter of life and death to you. It is easy to say you believe a rope to be strong and sound as long as you are merely using it to cord a box. But suppose you had to hang by that rope over a precipice. Wouldn't you then first discover how much you really trusted it?"

As painful as our losses are, they force us to a place that most of us would never voluntarily choose to go. As when Peter told Jesus that there was nowhere else to turn but to God or when I called out to God in a hospital emergency room all those years ago, there's only One to whom we can run when the unthinkable, unimaginable, unbearable happens.

In order to experience God's redemptive love and transforming power in our lives, we must acknowledge the extent of our losses. Acknowledging what we've lost—all the "might have beens"—allows us to move through the pain of our loss instead of getting lost in the midst of it. When we cry out to God, He hears us and comforts us.

Have Mercy

In Scripture we find many expressions of people crying out to God in the midst of their most painful moments. In Job, Lamentations, Ecclesiastes and Jeremiah, faithful believers expressed confusion, doubt and the pain of unbearable suffering. Also, consider that over a third of the psalms are prayers or songs written by people in pain. These inspired poems often express our pain for us when we can't find the words:

> Have mercy on me, LORD, for I am faint; heal me, LORD, for my bones are in agony. My soul is in deep anguish. How long, LORD, how long? . . .
> I am worn out from my groaning.
> All night long I flood my bed with weeping and drench my couch with tears. My eyes grow weak with sorrow; they fail because of all my foes (Ps. 6:2-3,6-7).

Can you relate to David's pain? When we're grieving, our pain saps the very energy out of us on every level. We become physically exhausted. We're emotionally drained. Our spirit feels battered and bruised from the blow. David makes it clear that he had cried so many tears that he couldn't cry any more. It's not that he didn't believe in God—he did. You may even recall that he was known as a man after God's own heart (see Acts 13:22). But even David couldn't understand why the God who had the power to change his circumstances, the One who had elevated him from being a simple shepherd boy to king of the nation, wouldn't do so.

When we cry out to God, even with our questions, our doubts and our raw emotion, we are respecting the enormity of what we've lost. When we cry out to Him, we are making ourselves vulnerable to the only One who really has the power to comfort, heal and restore us. We are relinquishing control so that He can take the reins of our lives. Keeping our volatile feelings and thoughts inside only creates an ongoing danger that will cause us to explode in a destructive outburst and hurt ourselves and others or implode into the darkness of depression and despair.

I know how strong Debra's faith was. I know that she loved me. I'm confident that she knew how much I loved her. As strange as it may sound, I honored her by crying out to God in the midst of my pain. I respected the depth of our commitment to one another by turning to the One who had brought us together in the first place.

You see, I'm convinced that our cries are a crucial and important step in the process of healing and restoration. If you haven't yet grieved your heart's heaviest losses, then now is the time. If you've stuffed your pain down into the recesses of your soul, then it's time to unpack. God can handle your pain. In fact, He makes it clear in His Word that He will never abandon us or forsake us. If you feel alone in your grief, you need to remember that there's One who's still there for you, who feels your pain just as deeply as you do. Draw close to God, and know that His arms will comfort you as nothing else will.

RESTORE AND RENEW

1. What's the most devastating loss you have had to endure? Where are you in the process of grieving and healing from this wound?

2. What are the other injuries and losses that continue to compound your suffering? How have you handled the cumulative weight of these burdens?
3. What do you want to tell God about what you've experienced through your loss? What would you like to have Him tell you?
4. How have you honored and respected the losses you have endured? Have you been able to find a way to express your thoughts, feelings and memories surrounding this loss?
5. Who can you share your grief with as you continue to heal and make room for God to restore you?

RECONNECT AND REVIVE

God, I'm simply wrecked when I think about all that I've lost. I don't understand why certain things have happened, and I can't imagine going forward when nothing will ever be the same. Give me the strength to acknowledge my pain and to release it to You so that I can experience Your comfort. Amen.

4

Heal with Hope: Treating Your Pain with God's Peace

If you've ever watched a brown chrysalis squirm and slowly begin to turn inside out, you know that a beautiful, colorful butterfly emerges from a cocoon. The same process occurs as baby birds break out of their shells, pushing and poking through the barrier that has contained their development to that point. In fact, all of nature experiences pain before new life occurs.

The same is true for you and me. It's a guarantee that comes from being human on planet Earth. No matter how wonderful our childhood may have been or how much we work to control circumstances so that we can avoid pain, heartache is still inevitable. Just as physical pain comes from having mortal bodies here, so too emotional pain comes with the territory of loving and being loved.

And truth be told, it's often more of a wilderness territory than an orderly, civilized structure. When we're hiking or camping in the wilderness, we face lots of unknowns—many of them dangerous. Bad weather, wild animals, poison ivy, flashfloods and wildfires all threaten to injure us and to end our journey. Similarly, we often encounter obstacles on our life's path that seem insurmountable: the loss of a loved one, a layoff at work, a financial crisis, a crippling disease. These barriers catch us off guard and leave us reeling with a new reality that seems literally beyond our imagination.

But God is present with us in these seemingly insurmountable physical and emotional trials. While we may not understand why He's allowed certain events to transpire or be able to imagine how He could ever redeem our devastating losses, God remains sovereign, good and loving. Like any caring parent, He hurts when His children hurt. And like the loving Father He is, God also longs to hold us, comfort us and bathe us in His peace that passes understanding.

Yes, there's no road map for avoiding pain, sidestepping loss or detouring around disappointment. But there is a way through it.

Why, Lord, Why?

Obviously, I experienced this kind of debilitating pain in the aftermath of losing my wife Debra. As I waited in the early morning hours of a sterile hospital room all those years ago, dozens of questions raced through my mind. Ultimately, they all amounted to "Why, Lord?" Why would God allow this to happen? Why would He seemingly disregard the prayers of all the hundreds—perhaps thousands—of people who had been quickly mobilized and were praying for my wife's recovery? Why, Lord, why?

When we're leveled by unexpected pain, we must do whatever it takes to keep communication lines open with God. If we need to scream, yell, cry, shout—whatever it is—He can handle it all. We must cling to Him and Him alone as our lifeline, calling out to Him in the midst of life's roaring current around us.

This was certainly my first impulse as the news of Debra's passing began to sink in. Basically, three strong outcomes emerged from my heart that night. First, I vowed to serve the Lord with greater intensity than ever before. I would not allow the enemy of my soul to win by crippling my faith and paralyzing my hope. Even though I didn't understand why God was allowing this to happen to me, I decided that I would trust Him on the journey that lay ahead.

Second, I asked the Lord for something. I prayed, "Whatever You do, Lord, please don't be silent." I knew that if I could just sense God's presence and hear Him speak to my heart then I would be okay. Like a child lost on a dark night, I knew that I could keep going as long as I could hear my Father's voice.

This request I made of the Lord was one I had made a few years earlier on behalf of friends of mine who had lost their two-year-old son to cerebral palsy. We had asked the Lord to please not be silent, and He had spoken to them in a dream that gave them a great measure of hope and encouragement. I had watched how the Lord had answered that request in their situation, and knowing that He is not a respecter of persons, I expected Him to speak to me as well.

And third, I made another request of the Lord: I prayed that Debra's death would not be in vain. I told the Lord that I needed to see evidence of Debra's impact on other people. I wanted help seeing how anything good could ever come of this huge loss. While God honored both my requests, I began to see Him responding to this second one within hours of my petition.

You see, I later learned that when I arrived at the hospital in the ambulance with Debra, about 10 people from our church were already there, praying and waiting at the trauma center. As the news spread each hour, the number of church members and friends continued to increase. So many gathered that they were moved from the ER waiting room to a small conference room, from a small conference room to a medium conference room, from a medium conference room to the largest conference room in the hospital. By the time the last person arrived, over 200 prayer warriors had gathered at the hospital.

My nurse that night said, "It's simply unbelievable! I've never seen anything like it. My life will never be the same after what I've seen here tonight. This outpouring of love is a testimony to your faith and to the church you attend." I had made just one phone call to my friend, Pastor Gordon Banks, while standing in the intersection where the accident had occurred. That one call unleashed a network into action that would carry me through the journey upon which I was about to embark.

Later, once I was released from the hospital, my church family immediately began to stop by my house to offer condolences. They told me that when the news of our accident and Debra's death was announced at our Wednesday night service, amazing things immediately began to happen. A mini revival was ignited. Those who had been at odds with each other or had fallen out of grace with one another because of business deals gone south began to confess their sins to each other and to repent for not walking with God as they should have been. There was hugging and crying and praying and laughing. Even in the midst of their grief and heartache, the Spirit of the Lord brought comfort to my church family.

Debra's death was clearly not going to be in vain.

God Is Able

As part of my commitment to God to serve Him more fervently than before, I knew that I needed some helpful habits to get me through the season ahead. The routine that I established after Debra's funeral would bring strength to me in the darkest night of my soul and become the anchor that would hold me firm to the Master of my destiny. It was very simple, really. It was simply a choice that no matter how bad I felt, before I did anything else each day, I would worship God, at least for a few minutes.

So every morning after waking up, I worshiped the Lord before doing anything else. Ron Kenoly was a popular Christian worship leader at that time and had released a CD entitled "God Is Able." His songs inspired and helped me in my belief that God is sovereign. And during that time I frequently reflected on what sovereignty actually means—not just that God is in control but that He is free from external control, imposed constraints and outside influences. As I contemplated this idea, I asked the Lord, "If You are free from external control, constraints and influences, then what determines Your choices with regard to us, Your children?"

As clearly as if God had audibly spoken the words, in my heart I heard, "My Word!"

When God releases His Word, He binds Himself to it and becomes the guarantor that the Word released will accomplish its intended purpose. So I reminded myself again of God's sovereignty, but now it seemed to hold a deeper meaning for me.

The songs on Ron Kenoly's CD helped me realize a significant truth about going forward. I realized that worship was going to be the catalyst that would enable me to take my eyes off my circumstances and keep them focused on the Lord. In worship I came to realize God's tenderness and gentle loving care for those who are completely broken and devastated. And it was clear to me that I wasn't the first—nor would I be the last—who experienced this kind of care.

Jeremiah the prophet describes an event that occurred when he was instructed by the Lord to go to the potter's house. As he watched the potter shape a vessel of clay in his hand, the clay became deformed. Calamities, distortions or setbacks while we are in the hand of the Master are neither fatal nor final. Why? Because the Potter has the ability to remold, reshape and refashion the clay so that the latter vessel is much more beautiful and valuable than the former vessel.

Yes, one day I had been walking with the Lord, a willing vessel confident of my future with the life partner with whom God had blessed me, and then, suddenly, I had been marred and broken, devastated beyond explanation, crushed into broken shards. Yet I was still in the Potter's hand. The Potter had His eyes on me, and He was ready to reveal Himself in ways never known to me before this event. It was when I understood this that I realized that the remolding and reshaping process had already begun in my life.

Let me encourage you that no matter what situation you find yourself in, if you have surrendered your life to Christ, you are in the Potter's hand. Though it may seem as if your circumstances are going to overtake you, don't be afraid, because the Lord is with you and is superintending the process of your life. In Him you will discover the power to persevere when you can't push through. Yes, you may not feel like worshiping Him. Yes, it will require all your effort some days to focus on Him and on the truth of His Word. But doing so will keep you going and growing forward.

You may experience some pain, but you will eventually come forth purified like fine gold. You will rise above the naysayers within and without. You will see the salvation of the Lord, and He will reveal Himself to you in ways that you have never known. Trust Him and be encouraged; stand still and see the salvation of the Lord! Stay in His presence through worship, and you will find strength in Him when you need it most.

Healing Starts Now

Worshiping the Lord throughout my grieving process was foundational to my restoration. It was, in fact, crucial, because it helped me realize another important choice that we have to make when we're wrestling with the painful process of our redemption. Shortly after Debra's funeral, God spoke a profound message to my heart, which in itself was a gift to me as He honored my request that He not be silent.

God said to me, "You can begin the healing process now or wait five years from now. Either way, you'll have to deal with the grief if you're going to move on with your life and fulfill the plan that I have for you." I knew that I didn't want to be a bumbling idiot five years from now, so I said to the Lord, "Do what You want to do in me. I will submit to whatever process You have designed for my life."

With my willingness to enter the process with Him beside me, God quickly led me to a place that truly defies description. Many dear friends and well wishers approached me after Debra's service, and apparently someone slipped a cassette into my hand, which I found the following week in my suit-coat pocket. It was Keith Staten's *Urban Praise: Worship in the House*, and it was definitely a divinely inspired gift.

Only God knew at the time how the songs on that CD would impact my life. Since my routine was to worship the Lord in the morning with music accompaniment, I started beginning my day with that cassette. Whereas Ron Kenoly's worship album affirmed the strength and sovereignty of God, Keith's worship album moved me to a place of trust in Him. It helped usher me into the secret place with songs like "Lord, I Thirst for You." The lyrics to that song read, "Lord, I thirst for You, and I long to be in Your presence. My soul will wait on You; Father, draw me nearer, draw me nearer, to the beauty of Your holiness. I will wait on You, Almighty God, in the beauty of Your holiness; I will worship You, Almighty God, in the beauty of Your holiness . . ."

I listened to this album morning, noon and night for the next two and a half months. The songs brought me into the "secret place" of God's presence (see Ps. 91:1, *KJV*), as spoken about in the Scripture. In this secret place I felt safe, protected and secure. The name "the secret place" made sense to me, because I didn't have physical directions to that place, nor did I ever know how or when I got there, but often I felt as if God had me tucked away someplace in Him. It was a place of complete solitude, a place where I could grieve deeply without being ridiculed or ashamed and could sit for hours in silence while He consoled me.

In this place I came to understand like never before just how much my heavenly Father really loved me—how much He loves us. As He nurtured and comforted me, it was in this place that I learned to embrace the struggle.

I pray that you are able to find this place when you need sanctuary from your life's storm. Here are the only directions I can give you: just cry out to the Lord. In His Word, God says, "If you look for me wholeheartedly, you will find me. I will be found by you" (Jer. 29:13-14, NLT). Similarly, the psalmist says, "For you are my hiding place; you protect me from trouble. You surround me with songs of victory" (Ps. 32:7, NLT).

God's presence was incredibly strong for me during this season, and I was more and more grateful that He did not forget my request after the dreadful night of the accident when I asked Him to speak to me. Time and time again He honored this request. He will do the same for you.

Perhaps you're in a place now in which you have been blindsided by your circumstances. Maybe your marriage has failed or your kids have broken your heart. The loss of a job or career has sent you reeling, searching for answers and putting you in a place of desperation. The word from the Lord is this: "Don't give up, and don't give in. Keep on holding on, because I'm about to do My greatest work in you."

Seeing Beyond the Blindside

As I share about my amazing times of intimacy with God, please don't think that I'm some kind of super saint or perfect Christian. I endured plenty of days when my soul cried out and I struggled just to make it through another hour, let alone the rest of a day. In fact, my grief was so intense some days that it literally made me feel sick to my stomach.

This gaping hole in my emotions made me question everything, not only about my past but about my future as well. I questioned whether I had built my life based upon a lie. I hadn't imagined that I wouldn't grow old with Debra. It had never crossed my mind that we wouldn't have children together. Nor did I ever think that she and I wouldn't share ministry around the world together. How could I have put my confidence and trust in what appeared to be a lie?

This very thought made me question everything about my future. How could I hope for a good one? Would I be willing to risk dreaming again, only to have my dreams shattered by circumstances beyond my control? How could I ever give my heart, my soul, my passion and my life to anyone ever again? This fear of attempting to live life to the fullest caused me to cry out to God, "What do I do now?"

Once again, my Father's answer surprised me. He said, "Keep moving forward! Nothing has changed."

His statement stunned me. I yelled at God, declaring, "What do you mean 'keep moving forward—nothing has changed'? *Everything* has changed!" Uncontrollable tears flooded my eyes as I wept and waited on the Lord to elaborate on His message to my heart. It felt like hours but was probably only a few minutes before I sensed God's compassion and was reminded of Romans 8:28: "All things work together for good to those who love God, to those who are the called according to His purpose" (*NKJV*).

God made it clear to me that nothing about the event that had unfolded in my life had changed His plan for me. He confirmed that I was still on course, still moving toward the ultimate destiny He had ordained for my life. Even though the plans that I had made were now thwarted, God's plan was still functioning and moving along according to schedule.

The Father's words comforted me, and I resolved that I would keep moving forward, trusting Him every step of the way. While many dark days still lay ahead for me, I was determined to face each one with courage and trust.

Making Room

I did several things over the months immediately following the accident that were pivotal to the healing process that I had submitted to shortly after Debra's funeral. Committing to morning worship was obviously one of them, as was communicating openly and honestly with God. I still struggled through some days, but I often felt a sense of peace even amidst the waves of sadness.

While it seemed minor at the time, getting rid of my television was a key decision that I made during that time. When I would arrive home in the evenings after a long day at work, I found myself numbingly flipping through the channels. Since Debra and I had chosen not to have cable, there were not a lot of channels to flip through. Realizing that I was wasting valuable time and just medicating the pain, I gave the TV to Goodwill after I couldn't find anyone who wanted to take it.

This one act allowed me to spend countless hours on my face in the living room. I cried for most of them; sometimes because of great sorrow and pain, other times because of the overwhelming love, comfort and peace that I felt from the Lord. I was either lying on my face in the carpet, spending time reading the Word and other inspirational books, or praying. This time with the Father was awesome and sweet; it was beautiful. I experienced an intimacy with the Lord that I hadn't known could even exist.

I'm going to explain something that may sound strange to some. As a matter of fact, what I experienced in my times with the Lord would have sounded a little strange to me if I hadn't walked the road I had been traveling.

During this time I gave myself completely over to God as I had not ever given myself to anyone or anything. Since I desperately needed more of Him and His presence in my life, I realized that I had to make even more room for Him. The more time I spent in the Lord's presence, the more I wanted to be in His presence. Each day brought me something new and refreshing along with a little more hope and strength. Each day allowed me to experience my heavenly Father in a way that caused me to know beyond a shadow of a doubt that He loved me and that I could trust Him.

One day during these months, as I was driving, I had a sudden awareness of God's presence with me. His compassionate message, once again, could not have been clearer: "*Allow* Me to comfort you." Without any explanation I knew exactly what He meant. During such times I felt the concentration of God's presence in a greater way than at other times. Soon His meaning became even clearer: "When you feel this greater concentration of My presence, stop what you are doing, and wait on Me." When I did as God told me, I would sense the Lord removing hurtful things from me and placing something new inside me that was the antithesis of what He had removed.

It was as if He said to me, "Ricky, let's make an exchange: your pain for My healing. Deal?" I didn't have to think about it. My weakness for His strength. My mourning for His gladness. My despair for His hope. My fear for His faith. My confusion for His clarity. My failure for His victory. My loneliness for His comfort. My past for His future.

I recognized that in order to make this exchange, I would have to first acknowledge my true feelings and not try to pretend that I was fine before my friends, family or church. Once I humbled myself by acknowledging my pain, only then could the Father and I make the exchange in order for Him to release healing.

So every day I began to acknowledge the state of my soul. When someone asked me how I was doing, if I was having a bad day, I would acknowledge it by saying, "I'm struggling today; I'm dealing with fear [or anger, confusion, hopelessness, despair, sadness, loneliness or apathy]." I would conclude the statement by saying, "Please pray for me." If I was having a good day, I would respond, "I'm doing okay today, but please continue to pray for me."

This response was necessary because of the emotional roller coaster that was a part of my daily routine. One moment I would be on a mountaintop with God, feeling good about my present situation. But within seconds of thinking that I was on top of the world, I would find myself in the pit of despair. I learned during that season not to take things one day at a time, because a day was too long. I learned to live moment by moment, because many times I was completely overwhelmed by my pain, sorrow and despair.

In the midst of it all, I made the exchange. Little by little, day by day, I was moving toward wholeness. God wants to turn our tears of mourning into the joy of dancing before Him. We only have to keep our heart open before Him.

Unpack Your Baggage

Habitually making this exchange with the Lord speeded my recovery process along in a way like nothing else I could have done. But there was one other situation that was quietly and stealthily working below the surface of my life. It was an enemy that I thought had been defeated by my first declarations on the night of Debra's departure.

When people asked me about the condition of the driver who had run the red light, my response was, "I haven't heard from him; however, I'm praying for him, and I forgive him, because he was just a puppet of the enemy." Deep within my soul I believed that since I couldn't bring Debra back, there was no need for me to hold this situation against this man; I figured that forgiveness was the only option. I had made that statement over and over to countless inquiries. The forgiveness issue had been settled the very night of Debra's death—or so I thought.

It was a wintry Tuesday evening about eight when I arrived home after having worked longer than usual at the church. After conducting leadership training, I was feeling confident that I had successfully pulled off one of my first meetings without Debra by my side. As I waited for leftover fried chicken and red beans and rice to warm, I picked up the mail.

Sifting through it, I came across a letter from the Denton County district attorney's office. I had been curious as to why the DA's office had not contacted me up until now, considering that the young man who had caused the accident had been charged with vehicular homicide. The letter began by saying that the case had been submitted to the Denton County grand jury by the district attorney's office. The grand jury's responsibility had been to weigh the evidence and to determine whether it justified the charge of vehicular homicide. The letter then stated that the grand jury had judged the information presented and had determined that the evidence "did not support the charge of vehicular homicide."

When I read that statement, a hot flash raced through my body. By the time I reached the end of the correspondence, I could feel the hair standing up on the back of my neck and steam blowing from my ears. I was appalled and shocked! What more did they need? This guy had a blood alcohol content level of .18, almost twice the legal limit at that time of .10—and because of it, my wife was dead! What kind of evidence spoke louder than that? I collapsed to my knees as my body shook with anger and despair while tears cascaded down my face. It was the first time that I had shouted at God since Debra's death.

Finally, the ironclad shell covering my heart had been lifted to reveal the true state of affairs. Yes, I was full of vitriol, anger and bitterness. If I could've gotten to that reckless driver in that moment, there's no telling what I would've done! My emotions, encased in Christian niceties for so long, led me to believe that I had settled the forgiveness question. Yet this letter made it clear I harbored rage, judgment and contempt in my heart for the one who had been responsible for the untimely death of Debra.

After 10 to 15 minutes of a complete emotional breakdown, I knew that I couldn't face this battle alone, and I called Gordon, my friend and fellow pastor. When he arrived, I was in a somewhat calmer state. Gordon's eyes welled up with tears as he read the letter, and he hung his head in disbelief. His ability to share my grief only fueled my return to an agitated state of anger and judgment.

Through tears, I said, "I want him to rot in jail." All I wanted at that instance was for this guy to pay for what he had done. He had taken two lives: Debra's as well as mine. Slumping into the soft cloth fabric of the sofa, I sobbed, "I just want justice."

We were silent for a few moments before Gordon spoke. "Ricky, I hurt for you right now. I'm sorry that you have to go through this. I can't understand why the grand jury has reached the conclusion that it has. But here's what I know: When man judges a matter, he might get it right, or he might get it wrong. Man is finite, and in judging matters he can only judge based upon the past and the present. He has no way of knowing if the present judgment is the right one or not; he doesn't know if the current judgment is going to help or destroy the one being judged."

He continued, "But when God judges a matter, He does so with full insight and knowledge. He knows the past, present and future, and He knows how His judgment is going to impact the person for the remainder of his life, even into eternity. Now you can harbor the bitterness and unforgiveness in your heart, and in that way you will judge this young man who caused the accident. However, you and I both know that the loser in this proposition will be you. We say that we want what God wants until what He wants is something that feels unbearable, and then we want what *we* want. Ricky, it's your choice—you be the judge, or let God be the judge."

I knew that what Gordon spoke was true, and I knew that I didn't want to live the rest of my life in bitterness and unforgiveness. I knew that I would be the one enslaved and that my anger would cause my future to spiral out of control and to be drowned in a miry pit of pain and despair. That night I acknowledged that I had not forgiven the drunk driver and in reality hated him. However, I wanted to maintain right standing with my heavenly Father, and I knew that forgiveness was the only path down which to travel.

Gordon and I prayed, and I asked the Lord to help me overcome my feelings of hatred and unforgiveness. The presence of the Lord filled the living room, and I felt as if a thousand pounds had been lifted off my shoulders. I thanked Gordon for his time and advice and told him that I would give him an update after I spoke with the DA for clarification regarding the grand jury's decision.

The next morning I called the District Attorney's office as soon as it opened. I explained to the receptionist that I had received a letter in the mail about a grand jury ruling, and I summarized the accident. After going through several "Wait" and "Please hold" responses, before each of which I had to repeat my inquiry, I finally got through to an attorney who gave me a response. He came on the line and said, "Mr. Texada, we're so sorry for the delay in responding to your inquiry. However, we've searched our files and discovered that your wife's case has not even been assigned to an attorney in our office yet. We're not exactly sure how you received this letter with our seal on it."

No one had an explanation for how a letter could have been generated with no case number assigned to it and no actual grand jury hearing. But it was clear to me. I realized that this was the hand of God. The Father had revealed Himself again. As I hung up the phone, I chuckled and pointed my finger toward heaven and said, "You got me again! Thank You for revealing my heart to me!"

When we carry the heavy baggage of anger, resentment, unforgiveness, hatred, bitterness and resentment inside us, we don't have room for God's peace. The weight of our unexpressed emotions burdens us beyond our ability to grieve and to accept the comfort and restoration God wants to give. That letter from the

DA's office was a divine catalyst that forced me to acknowledge what I had been working hard to keep under wraps. But the Lord knew that I couldn't experience the full process of restoration without unpacking my baggage first.

The Power of Peace

Six months after our accident, I wrote in my journal, "I'm no longer grieving, though I miss Debra terribly." Even though I couldn't see a plan for my future, I now felt hopeful. At one time, shortly after Debra's death, remarriage for me had been out of the question. I had felt this primarily for two reasons: First, I wondered whether I could ever love a woman as much as I loved Debra, and second, I was afraid to allow myself to ever again go emotionally and mentally as deeply as I had in my relationship with Debra.

The pain of her loss was more than I could bear, and I wasn't certain I ever wanted to risk going there again. Because of that, my plan was to take the apostle Paul's admonition to remain single and not seek to be married. I was now single, and my focus was to understand why the Lord had allowed my life to be spared in the accident.

When Debra died, I felt like a blind man with no direction. For a while I couldn't see my way. I became uncertain about the calling that the Lord had placed on my life and whether I could really hear His voice. I was definitely concerned about my future, yet I was determined to hold onto God's hand so that wherever He led, I would follow. And the Lord clearly led me through days that I could never have endured alone. He helped me to surrender to supernatural peace, to forgive the man responsible for my wife's death, and to grow closer to Him in ways I could never have experienced otherwise.

No matter what you're going through, you have the same opportunity. If you want to experience God's gifts, then you must listen to His voice and follow His guidance. Maintaining and restoring your trust in Him requires listening for His voice, accepting His provision, and making room for Him in your life. Even when you don't understand your losses, even when nothing about your life makes sense, you must never forget the solid rock of God's love for you. He is for you, even when that feels impossible to believe. He will see you through this process of growth, this transformation from a painful struggle into the flight of a beautiful creature with new wings.

RESTORE AND RENEW

1. How have you experienced God's presence during seasons of loss or grief? How have you seen His hand at work in your life this week?
2. What stops you from trusting God completely and fully for your healing and restoration? Have you been honest with Him about your struggles to trust Him?
3. Who are the people you need to forgive in order to move forward with your restoration? Who are the people you need to ask to forgive you?
4. What evidence of growth have you glimpsed in your own life most recently? Where do you sense change is occurring—in your relationships, prayer time, energy level? Something else?

RECONNECT AND REVIVE

Dear Father, I want to trust You and grow closer to You. I open my heart to You and ask that You would give me ongoing reminders of Your presence. Thank You for not abandoning or forsaking me. Amen.

5

Accept His Assurance: Experiencing God's Supernatural Comfort

Like most parents, Cyd and I try to teach our boys about the value of earning and appreciating what they have. We like surprising them with toys and gadgets that they like, and we often do this at birthdays and Christmas, but we also want our sons to understand the process of acquiring something significant. We encourage them to save their allowance and other money they receive as gifts and to handle their funds wisely. If there's a big-ticket item they're saving to purchase, we encourage them to practice patience and to celebrate each milestone of their financial goal that they save along the way.

Sometimes during the process of restoration, I wonder if our heavenly Father wants us to learn a similar kind of lesson. Not necessarily about material possessions as much as about encouragement from the Lord in things such as conversations with friends or even signs and wonders—as well as the supernatural comfort that comes from them—about our healing. While the why questions may never be answered the way we hope they will, God often responds to our requests for answers in amazing ways. As answered prayers and divine revelations begin to accumulate, we can find ourselves recognizing our Father's fingerprints.

Part of the reason for this may be that we are more receptive during times of grief. After we've lost someone or something precious to us, we often become more sensitive to God's supernatural intervention. Maybe we're hoping that we'll wake up from a very bad dream and discover that everything is as it used to be. Maybe we're hoping for a miracle, the kind that defies logic, probability and possibility. While God certainly can provide a miracle cure, restoration or healing for us and our loved ones, usually He leads us through more of an ongoing process than causing an instantaneous moment of complete change.

Dreams were a significant part of my restoration as I recovered from losing Debra and tried to regain my footing. Certainly prayers and incredibly well-timed support from other people also played a huge role. And there were enough "coincidences" of confirmation that I knew that God was involved and directly meeting my needs and responding to my painful questions.

I've shared a few of these with you already, but in this chapter I'd like to share a few more—ones that may sound a little far-fetched or unbelievable. I reveal them to you here not because you should expect the exact same kind of supernatural dreams and occurrences but because you should expect God's supernatural assurance and peace beyond understanding to penetrate your life.

Heaven or Earth

The night of the accident, I had to wait in the ER most of the early morning hours until a regular hospital room became available. Of all the questions floating through my mind, one repeatedly surfaced: "Lord, how could You disregard the prayers of all those people in the waiting room—and around the world? The people praying for us to be okay, for Debra to live, for my injuries to be healed?" My understanding of God as my heavenly Father had always included the assurance that He hears the prayers of His people. It didn't make sense to me that so many hundreds if not thousands of other believers could be praying and God would not act to answer them accordingly.

But sitting there in the early hours of the morning, dazed and overwhelmed, I finally heard Him speak to my heart and answer my nagging question.

The Lord replied to me, "I didn't disregard those prayers—Debra had a choice to remain on the earth or to come to heaven."

Now this may sound totally crazy to you, but I have no doubt in my mind that it was God conversing with my troubled heart. As I pondered His response over and over again, I could make no sense of it. Debra had a choice? Debra had a choice! Debra had a choice?! So I asked the Lord, "How could that be? How could she have had a choice and not chosen to be here by my side?"

Debra had received five skull fractures, apparently from being tossed around the car's interior after the impact from the drunken driver's car; she should have died instantly. Though she was never conscious after the impact, I knew that she had lived almost three hours after we were hit. God said to me, "What seemed like three hours in your realm was only seconds in mine. As she was making her decision to stay on the earth or come home, Debra was concerned about three things."

I couldn't believe this strange conversation, but I also knew that what the Lord was telling me was true.

God continued, "The first question Debra asked Me was, 'How's Ricky going to make it?' I showed her a glimpse of your future, and she was satisfied. Her second question was, 'How's my family going to make it?' So I showed her a glimpse of her family's future, and she was satisfied. Her third question was, 'How's Covenant Church going to make it?' and I showed her a glimpse of Covenant Church's future, and she was satisfied. Debra said, 'I'm done. I'm not staying here on the earth—I'm coming home to heaven!'"

Even as God's explanation flooded my heart and mind, I struggled to grasp this message and only came up with more questions. Why would she do that? Didn't she love me enough to stay? Was it selfish on her part to choose to leave for heaven? Was I being selfish for wanting her to remain in this stress- and conflict-filled world?

Then the Lord reminded me of the conversation between Debra, Pastor Kathy and me that we'd had in Debra's office two weeks before the accident. Debra and I always gave gifts to our leaders at Christmas time to thank them for their faithful service throughout the year. That year we had chosen a book written by Jesse Duplantis titled *Close Encounters of the God Kind*, which chronicled his account of his visit to heaven. It seemed appropriate, because it would inspire and encourage our leaders, and Debra, for an unknown reason, was fascinated with heaven. Even though we had over 150 leaders to give books to, we were determined to write a brief word of encouragement on the inside cover of each book.

In Debra's office that day, with books stacked 10 high on any surface not covered, we were signing the books when Pastor Kathy stepped into the office. She said, "I've heard that you all were personally signing books for our leaders. What a fantastic gift!" She then picked up a book, flipped through it and paused, clearly reflecting on some thought. "I wonder why God allows some people to see heaven and doesn't let others see it?" she said.

Without hesitation I promptly exclaimed, "I know why God won't let Debra see heaven! If she sees it, she's not coming back!"

My unknowingly prophetic words had come true. No doubt my wife had seen heaven, and the choice for her was crystal clear. Tears streamed down my face there in the hospital room. How could I blame Debra for wanting to be with the Lord in the beauty of heaven? Though questions still ran through my mind, I knew without a doubt that the Lord had pulled back the veil and was beginning to let me see what He was up to.

God Is Not Silent

As you've already read, a mini revival had broken out at our church during the Wednesday evening service following Debra's death. But I didn't tell you everything. David and Claudia Albrecht were one of the couples to visit my home after that service, and what they told me assured me that I really had heard from the Lord about Debra having a choice to stay in heaven or to come back to the earth.

That night when they visited, they asked me if I had heard what Pastor Ralph Holland had shared with the congregation earlier that evening, and of course I hadn't. He'd told the church that he had been in the hospital room with Pastors Mike and Gordon when Pastor Mike had leaned over to Debra and whispered in her ear, "Debra, if you want to pull through this, we'll fight and believe God to raise you up. But if you want to go home, we release you."

Pastor Ralph had then seen something absolutely unbelievable. He said that after Pastor Mike presented the choice to Debra, he saw Debra's spirit sit up. As he rubbed his eyes a few times to make sure his eyes weren't playing a trick on him, he looked again and saw Debra's physical body remain prone on the hospital bed, while her spirit was sitting up, dressed in a white robe. His first thought was that she was more beautiful than he had ever seen her. Debra's spirit made a motion as if to smooth out a wrinkle from her robe, then departed from her body.

David indicated that Pastor Ralph was hesitant to tell the story, because he didn't want others to think that he was trying to exploit the emotional state of the people. You can't imagine how I felt when I heard this story. I began to cry, because now I knew that God was not going to be silent.

That same night Dave and Claudia also shared with me how they had seen Debra and me working so diligently in the church. They commended me for our sacrificial lifestyle and our passion for helping people. They confessed that they had been on the sidelines and not engaged in the battle to advance the kingdom of God. They pledged that they would get in the fight and make their lives count in memory of Debra.

The Albrechts became small-group leaders, enrolled in and graduated from Christ for the Nations and today are pastors of a church in the nation of Nicaragua. Debra's death was not in vain, and the Lord was not being silent. He continued to speak clearly in unmistakable ways to respond to my request.

Answered Prayer

God continued to answer my prayers and to make it clear that He had not abandoned me. If I had withdrawn from Him and refused to listen or to look at all that He shared, I would have missed out on many enormous blessings and moments of reassurance. It might sound strange, but in your life, just as He did in mine, God has already started the process of transforming your heartache into the soil for new life.

Another little but important response from God comes to my mind. Debra's dad, Peter, and I had made the decision to return Debra's body to her hometown of Morrow, Louisiana; but before we did so, we planned to have a memorial service for her at Covenant Church. I had been told by the funeral director, however, that because of Debra's extensive head injuries and because of the amount of time it had taken us to get her body from the hospital, we probably would not be able to have the casket open at the memorial service.

Needless to say, I was troubled and disappointed, in large part because I knew how important an open casket was to Debra's mother, Eunice Smith, who had come from Louisiana. Debra's father, Peter, had remained home because he couldn't bear the thought of even coming to Dallas, let alone seeing his daughter's body. He also had to make the arrangements there in Morrow.

Debra's mom was a kind and caring woman. She had worked for years at the local hospital in Bunkie, Louisiana, where she was in charge of housekeeping for the operating rooms. She was perfect for the position as she was so conscientious and loved everyone and was in turn loved by everyone she met.

Debra's mom always referred to her children, along with their spouses, as her "baaabies." Naturally, she wanted to see Debra as badly as any mother would. She kept asking me over and over, "Did she suffer any?" I knew that she was trying to process the events that had unfolded so suddenly in her youngest daughter and second youngest child's life. I assured her time and time again that Debra was never conscious after the accident occurred.

Eunice became distraught when she heard the news about the high probability of a closed casket. Having already seen the hand of the Lord through hearing Pastor Ralph's testimony, I prayed fervently for God to intervene by granting Eunice her one last request. "Please, Lord," I prayed, "allow Debra's mom to see her daughter's face one last time."

My prayer was heard and answered. The day before the scheduled memorial service, the funeral director called to inform me that we would be able to view the body an hour before the memorial service to determine if the casket would be open or closed. There was expectancy in my heart that the Lord would not be silent, and He continued to confirm His presence.

The memorial service was held on December 20 at 11 in the morning. Debra's family and I arrived about a quarter to 10. The funeral director and his staff were preparing the casket. We walked slowly down that middle aisle of Covenant Church. Never in a million years up to this point had I ever entertained the thought that I would be burying a loved one in this church, let alone the wife of my youth.

The casket was open when we began to walk toward Debra's body. I couldn't believe what I was seeing; a glow seemed to radiate from the casket. As we looked down upon Debra lying there, no one could keep from crying. Our tears were tears of pain and tears of joy. Her mother commented through the tears, "Isn't she so beautiful!" We all agreed that an open-casket ceremony was appropriate.

God had done it again. He had answered my prayer; He had not been silent. Through something so simple and yet so meaningful, He kept saying to me, "I'm here."

Preparing for the Unimaginable

I know that these answered prayers and moments of divine revelation may sound strange and over the top—even I think so sometimes. But I also know the mysterious and powerful ways in which God can work. And when we are aching with grief and struggling to get our bearings during a major trial, He will find ways—large and small—to remind us of His presence, His love and His sovereignty.

Two weeks after Debra's death, reports continued to come in from a variety of people who all confirmed that Debra had been preparing for her departure in some unconscious way. The same kinds of memories and conversations continued drifting through my mind as well. For instance, as Debra and I had been in the midst of remodeling our home six months before the accident, she had mentioned that she felt as though we were preparing it for someone else to live there. I never thought twice about it at the time she said it. But now moments like those haunted me with their divine foresight.

And my memories were not the only ones. In August, as the membership services director at our church, Debra had begun training her replacement, Brenda Hansen. The training process had called for Debra to relinquish her role as director in April. Shortly before her death in December, she had come to the trainee and said, "Membership Services is now your responsibility—you're ready."

It was about this same time that Kim Clement, a prophet ministering at Covenant Church, had called Brenda out of the audience. Kim had proceeded to tell Brenda that in two weeks God would suddenly elevate her to a new level. Debra's accident occurred two weeks to the day of the prophetic word.

Debra had also told our administrative assistant, Alycia Sosa, a week before she passed, "Make sure you take good care of Ricky, because he's your responsibility now." She laughed about it then, but now it seemed almost eerie.

My sister, Tammie, described to me how Debra had shared with her during the week of Thanksgiving that she had taken me as far as she could and that it was now time for her to step out of the way. Tammie admitted that she hadn't really understood what Debra had meant or even given much thought to it until Debra was gone.

Becky Pierce, one of the women Debra had asked to pray for us regarding having children, told me that around two weeks before she died, Debra had come to her and made a strange request that she stop praying about that issue. When Becky inquired as to why, Debra simply said, "It's just not that important anymore." I'd had no idea she'd told Becky that, and to my knowledge, we'd both still wanted kids.

More than Can Be Imagined

Debra and I participated in many ministry areas during our tenure at Covenant Church. No ministry area was as much fun and as energizing as working with the two-year-olds in the church's nursery department. We volunteered in that area as a way of "paying it forward," believing that one day we would have children of our own in the nursery. Because we had no children, at the time of her death an agonizing pain pierced my heart. The night of December 30, days after Debra's death, would change my perception forever as the Lord spoke to me through a dream.

In the dream, I found myself standing in a room with many of our friends. However, Debra was not in the room. As I inquired about her whereabouts, I was told that she had just left the building and was going to another place where more of our friends had congregated. When I arrived at the second location, I was informed that she had just left and was going to another place. As I began to drive to the third location, I felt frustrated and I thought to myself, *Why does Debra keep leaving? She knows that I'm looking for her.*

Finally, arriving at the third place where Debra was supposed to be, I opened the door to the building and what I saw took me by surprise: There was Debra sitting in a chair with her back to the door. All around her were children who were laughing and singing; they were surrounded by arts and crafts supplies. Apparently, Debra had been teaching them about Jesus because one child after another would run up to her and say, "Look, Ms. Debra! See my picture of Jesus; thank you for teaching us about Jesus." Debra was filled with joy and laughter as she entertained each one and commented on his or her display of artwork. This moment was so tender and special that I began to quietly weep; I knew in this moment that I could not interrupt what was taking place, so I slowly and softly closed the door. At that moment, I woke up! The tears from my dream were now streaming down my face as I whispered, "So that's what Debra is doing in heaven . . . she's working with children." Knowing that this dream was so real that it had to be the Lord speaking to me, I asked Him to confirm what I had just witnessed.

The next day at church I was approached by Donna Yourney, a dear friend of ours. As she drew near me, I noticed the biggest smile on her face and wondered what she was so happy about. She looked me in the eyes with such sincerity and said, "I want you to know that I had a dream about Debra last night. In my dream I saw her in heaven working with children!" When she said that, the joy of the Lord surged through my emotions as I began to profusely thank the Lord for giving Donna the same dream that I had on the same night. No doubt God had confirmed my dream and Debra had more children than she ever imagined.

Freedom Behind Bars

On New Year's Day, as I was thinking about these stories and the dream of Debra in heaven, the phone rang. It was a collect call from Debra's brother, Patrick.

Patrick was Debra's third oldest brother, and he had been incarcerated in Angola State Penitentiary since 1984. Angola, known as one of the toughest prisons in the United States, is situated between the Louisiana swamps and the rattlesnake-infested woods along the Mississippi River. Patrick, a handsome man with smooth yellow skin, a low, well-edged haircut and a charming smile, is built like a linebacker at six feet two and 235 pounds. He's the type of guy who either liked a person or didn't and had no problem telling people where they stood with him. He had vowed to never let prison break him, and because of that he'd spent a lot of time in solitary confinement. Though his exterior appearance read "tough, kick-butt and take names," I knew that deep within he was as tenderhearted and generous as his sister had been.

Debra, her family and I had visited Patrick at Thanksgiving, just weeks before her death. She and I had left the prison really concerned for him. Patrick knew that we were Christians and had always respected us by trying to be on his best behavior around us—not cursing, telling dirty jokes or being crude in any way. But that last visit had been different: He had cursed liberally, told us shocking stories about prison life and presented an "I don't care" attitude about life in general. Although Debra and I had prayed for years that Patrick would have an encounter with God, after that visit we earnestly prayed for him more than ever.

I accepted the call as we had done for a number of years; I was glad to hear from him and gave Patrick an update on how things were going with me. I told him about the dreams and the confirmation I had received, and we both chuckled regarding our memories of Debra. Then he changed the subject: "I have a question for you, Ricky. What is this speaking in tongues stuff all about?"

Patrick knew that Debra and I had experienced the fullness of the Holy Spirit in this way, so I inquired as to whether something had happened to inspire his question. "Yes," he said and began to tell me about it. He had been invited by one of his friends to attend a chapel service held in the prison. At first he had been reluctant, because he didn't believe in putting on airs with God if he wasn't serious. However, Debra's death had deeply wounded him, and whenever he thought about her, he cried. With further prodding, he had agreed to attend the service.

The minister sharing that day happened to be a woman, and he was cool with that. After she finished sharing her message, she extended an invitation for the inmates to give their hearts to Jesus. Patrick said to me that he had neither the desire nor the intention to respond to the call except for the fact that the minister zeroed in on him, and he was already broken by Debra's death.

She spoke to him and said, "Hey you, you big red fella, you need to get down here at this altar." Patrick was stunned by the fact that she would single him out. Typically, he would have felt that this was an act of disrespect. Yet like a little lamb, he slowly stood up and stepped forward. He said, "I walked to the front of the room, and the woman began to pray for me. Then she did what she was not supposed to do. She placed her forehead on my chin and her hand on top of my head. As she began to pray, I became dizzy, and the room began to spin. The next thing I knew I was flat on my back. When I gathered my senses, I was speaking in tongues. What happened to me, Ricky?"

Through the laughter and tears, I began to give him the biblical explanation of his divine encounter. Patrick then acknowledged that he was going to study his Bible and walk with the Lord with everything he had in him. When I asked about his motivation, he paused for a moment and then said softly, "I want to see my little sister again." Consequently, he had given his heart to the Lord and started attending Bible studies and taking correspondence courses to grow in his knowledge of the Lord.

We talked quite awhile that day and concluded our conversation with prayer. As he prepared to hang up the phone, he said, "I love you, bro!" For Patrick to say that to any man was nothing short of a miracle! I knew that Debra was celebrating and rejoicing like crazy up in heaven.

In fact, the Lord reminded me of the conversation between Him and me that night in the hospital. He had revealed to me that Debra had asked Him how her family would fare if she stayed in heaven. I believe she saw Patrick coming into the kingdom—if her life was planted as a seed in the ground—and she knew that Patrick would be a part of the fruit coming forth from her death.

A Shot in the Arm

My confidence in God's plan for me was growing with each testimony unfolding all around. I called each little revelation and event a shot in the arm. Each of them was a little unexpected gift that lifted my spirits, and they always came at just the right time, when I needed encouragement the most. A few days after my conversation with Patrick and several weeks after Debra's death, another shot in the arm took God's presence in my life to a whole new level.

I went to bed one evening as I did any other night; I was finally starting to sleep more as I had before the accident. That night I dreamed that I was back in my hometown, on the bayou, as locals call the little country community where I was raised. I was in the front yard at the home of my great uncle and aunt, "Pop" and "Aunt Too Sweet."

I had grown up with them, so it wasn't strange that my dream was set in their yard. Because all the parents along the bayou worked, Pop and Aunt Too Sweet were charged with the responsibility of keeping an eye on all the neighborhood kids during the summer. They were also the bedrock of our little church, Second Evening Star Missionary Baptist Church.

Their residential lot was elevated about five feet above the surface of the street. In the middle of the lot on the edge of a hill was a massive 100-year-old-plus pecan tree. Slightly toward the eastern property line, near the driveway, was a giant ponderosa pine.

Whenever we kids sat under that towering pecan tree on those hot and steamy summer days, Pop and Aunt Too Sweet would drill their wisdom into us, telling us things like, "Keep the Lord first in your life" and "Get an education." Another mantra of theirs was "Keep on keeping on." In other words, "Don't get stuck and stop trying to move forward in life. If things aren't going well, don't let it stop you completely. Sure, life has many surprises and setbacks, but with the Lord on your side, you can always keep on keeping on."

In the dream I began walking from their driveway toward the street, when Debra appeared by my right side. I paused and turned toward her. It seemed as if a sunbeam was shining directly on her face. A cool breeze was rustling through the needles on the pine. Her big beautiful brown eyes glistened as she warmly smiled. I broke the silence and asked, "Debra, why did you have to go?"

She simply looked at me and encouragingly said, "Ricky, you can make it!" She kept smiling, and she repeated this same statement two more times. When I awakened with a deep peace over me, I thought to myself, *She's telling me to keep on keeping on. Don't stop now—life must continue.*

This message may not come to you in your dreams, but if you're in the process of restoration, then you need to hear it. You may not know why things have happened or what God's up to in your situation. You may wonder if God still loves you as you once thought He did. You might even be struggling to believe that He can be trusted. Whether you've lost a loved one, a job, your reputation or your retirement savings, you must not become paralyzed by your grief. Imagine God telling you what Debra told me: "You can make it! Don't give up, and don't give in. Keep on holding on, because I'm about to do My greatest work in you."

Sweet Dreams

I knew that the dream was a word from the Lord for me, and He confirmed that to me the very next day. It was the first Sunday of the New Year. Again, I cried during most of the service because of my loneliness and uncertainty. After 15 years of being in church with Debra, it was so hard to be there and not have her by my side. Nevertheless, the pain I experienced was eased by the overwhelming love being shown to me by God's people and by His manifest presence strengthening and encouraging me.

At the end of the service, a close friend of ours, Kim Atkinson, came up and asked me how I was doing. She hugged me in support and then began to describe a dream she'd had the previous night. She told me that the dream had taken place inside Covenant Church. In the dream she saw Debra and me in the same room; however, the room was divided by a transparent partition. Kim could see us both, but Debra and I couldn't see each other. Kim then tried to give Debra a bundle of Life Teams related papers, but Debra said to her three times, "Give it to Ricky—he knows what to do."

I couldn't believe it—another divine confirmation! Because Debra had been such a great administrator as the director of small-group ministry, I'd never had to worry about administrative details.

Her skills had allowed me to develop in my leadership gifts while she handled the detailed administrative matters. This dream relayed to me that I could handle the area that I usually delegated to her. Kim's dream gave me confidence that I could handle whatever I faced as it related to the small-group ministry at Covenant Church.

No Ordinary Ordination

The Father's words comforted me, and I resolved that I would keep moving forward, trusting Him every step of the way. Many dark days lay ahead for me, but I was determined to face each one with courage and trust. As I embarked on this new season, one of the most significant days was my pastoral ordination on February 9. That morning, about six weeks after the accident, I awakened with a great sense of expectancy as well as deep sorrow. The ordination would be the culmination of a long journey that had started over a decade prior in Baton Rouge, Louisiana.

In the spring of 1986, my senior year of college, I had begun to attend a church pastored by Reverend Wilbur Scott, whom I had met through Debra. Reverend Scott was the pastor of a church near the community in which Debra had grown up. He had experienced an amazing encounter with the Holy Spirit and subsequently started a church in Scotlandville, the neighborhood just outside the university campus. I had agreed to join him in establishing the work by serving on the worship team and occasionally teaching in the mid-week service.

During one of the revivals hosted by the church, a prophet from Arkansas had come as the guest speaker—a white preacher who had come to minister in an all-black congregation in the heart of a black neighborhood. During one of the services, he called me out and gave me a prophetic word. He said, "The hand of the Lord is upon you, and the Lord has called you to do great things for Him. The Lord is your teacher, and you won't need anyone to teach you the Word of God, for He will teach you Himself." But what really stood out was his next statement: "The Lord is calling you out, and you will become a pastor at a large white church."

When that word was delivered, I said to the Lord, "Whatever You want me to do, I will do it; and if that's Your will, if You open the door, then I will walk through it." I didn't know if the prophet meant that the church building would be white, the members of the congregation would be predominately white, or the pastor would be white. Only God knew.

But on that February morning 11 years later, I found out. I was about to be ordained into the ministry by a white pastor as a member of his pastoral team at a church whose members were predominantly white and whose building was largely white! I was excited, humbled and honored that the Lord and Pastors Mike and Kathy Hayes would bestow such a privilege upon me. I had mixed emotions, however, because Debra was supposed to be standing next to me.

Pastor Mike had come into our office six weeks earlier to announce that our ordination was scheduled sometime at the beginning of the new year. Now his words were about to be fulfilled; the only exception was that Debra was not standing next to me. The bittersweetness of this day was unavoidable, but with my family and members of Debra's family present for the ordination, it made the burden that I was carrying a little lighter.

The worship that day was intense and exuberant! The choir sang and people rejoiced as I had never seen since the first day I had set foot in Covenant Church in 1988. The presence of the Lord was so strong that I could feel the thickness and weightiness of His presence in the atmosphere. Then it was time.

All the pastors were on stage with Pastors Mike and Kathy Hayes. Dressed in a new tailored black suit, a gift from the church, I walked slowly up the seven steps to the top of the platform with tears streaming down my face. I looked into Pastor Mike's and Pastor Kathy's eyes, which were filled with tears and deep compassion. Pastor Mike approvingly nodded as I approached him at the center of the stage. By now it seemed as if every pastor and member in the congregation was wiping tears from their eyes. I felt the Lord place a heavy garment on me as I knelt before Pastors Mike and Kathy. With my hands raised high above me in worship to the Lord, Pastor Mike began to pray over me.

My eyes were closed when I felt a warm sensation touch the top of my head, and a strong sweet smell enveloped my nostrils. Something began to trickle down my face. Pastor Mike had taken the *entire* flask of anointing oil, not just a few drops, and poured it on my head, completely saturating me. He then pulled out a prestigious sword and with it touched my right shoulder and then my left. It was the first time to my knowledge that he had ever used a sword for an ordination service.

As I stood to hug him, the church released a thunderous shout and applause. I was now a pastor, an ordained minister of the gospel of Jesus Christ. In that moment all the cares, fears and pain dissipated, and we rejoiced in God's faithfulness. There are many congratulations and stories that could be told about that day. One of those stories was told to me by one of our life team leaders, Austin Aniebue.

Austin shared with me an event that had occurred before the start of the church service on my ordination day. He said that he had walked into the sanctuary and immediately sensed an almost tangible presence of the Lord in the atmosphere. When he had sat down in a pew, to his amazement he had seen an angel about 12 feet tall standing to the right of the stage. In the angel's right hand had been a large sword. The angel had taken the sword and hurled it toward the center of the stage. Austin said that the sword had landed in the very spot where I had knelt during the ordination ceremony.

It wasn't until the ordination service began that Austin understood what he had seen. He was amazed when Pastor Mike pulled out a sword as a part of the ordination ceremony. God had been faithful to His word: I was ordained at a large church whose senior pastor as well as members were predominately white and whose building was constructed of large white stones. God had been more than faithful!

Fast and Furious

Fast forward to August 17 to another church service equally instrumental in my healing and restoration. While watching a video during this service of a special ceremony that Pastors Kathy Hayes and Derozette Banks had attended in Washington, DC, I was given a glimpse of myself in the future. In this vision I was powerful yet humble, passionate but purposeful, determined and not distracted. I was not intimidated by what I saw; however, I became keenly aware that there had to be a total transformation of who I was in order to fulfill this purpose to which I was being called.

In my desperation, as I sat on the front row pew, I called out to God, "Lord, the man I see and the man I am are not the same man. There must be a transformation in me if I am to accomplish Your purposes and plans. Change my mind and my perspective. Allow me to see people, places, things and situations as You do. Help me to love and to be compassionate as You are. Also, Lord, please take off my old garments and put new garments on me."

In Bible times garments represented identity and lifestyle; by them people could determine an individual's family, educational status, occupation, and more. I concluded my prayer by saying, "I won't eat another bite of food until You do this. If I show up in heaven before my time and You ask me why I am there, I'll just say, 'You didn't change me.'" Unless I could fulfill the Lord's purposes and plans, I didn't care about living. The person who had represented my future on this side of eternity was already in heaven. So heaven was very real to me.

I didn't say a word to anyone about what had transpired for me during that service. As I left the building, I sensed the presence of God all over me. I gathered that Moses, Elijah and Jesus must have felt the same way as they embarked upon an extended fast.

Days one through six of my fast passed without incident. I had no desire for food of any sort. I drank a couple glasses of apple juice each day. However, on day seven, one week later, I found myself back in church again. No one knew anything about the request I had made to God in the silence of my heart one week earlier. All the pastors and their wives gathered in the green room before service, as was our custom, for prayer. I was the only single pastor then on staff. Pastor Mike was standing to my right as we stood in a big circle that enveloped the entire room. With his eyes closed he began to groan as if wrestling with a terrible burden.

I thought to myself, *I have never seen Pastor Mike act this way before a service. He is really going to preach the roof off this morning, and I can't wait to hear it.* Then, to my surprise, he opened his eyes, turned toward me and said, "Ricky, I have a word from the Lord for you." He spoke the following words:

The past was good, but the future is better; and when you look back on the past, there is no more pain, because you have allowed the joy of the Lord to become your strength. The Lord says He has heard your cry, and He is going to give you a mind like His. He is changing your perspective, and you will see people, circumstances, things and situations the way He sees them. He is taking off the old garments and putting on a new garment. The Lords says to you, "Do not be afraid about your future, because your future is secure in Me. I know the plans I have for you, plans to prosper you, and not to harm you, plans to give you hope and a future. For I am the Lord, and I declare this to be a day of new beginnings for you."

From the very first moment Pastor said, "I have a word from the Lord for you," tears started streaming down my face. But when he began to declare that the Lord was giving me His perspective and taking the old garments off, I completely lost it. It was as if a river of tears burst forth out of me. As I mentioned, I hadn't told anyone of my request or that I was fasting for transformation. I knew that the Lord was really speaking. I knew that I had His ear, and I believed everything that He declared to me through Pastor Mike. My heart was bursting with joy as I glanced around the room and noticed that everyone was crying, hugging and rejoicing.

In that moment of incredible life, I asked Pastor Mike if he knew what day it was. He said no. I told him, "It's the eight-month anniversary of the accident that resulted in Debra's death."

He said, "My, my, the number eight in Scripture represents new beginnings!"

And that's exactly what the Lord had just declared over me through Pastor Mike's words: new beginnings!

The Lord can do the same for you. His encouragement to you may not involve prophetic visions, powerful dreams or the kind of objective confirmation I experienced. But if you spend time with Him, when you release your sorrow, fear and pain into His care, you can rest assured that He will make His presence known to you. He may only give you a comforting feeling, one that you can't explain given the suffering you're going through, or a serene sense that somehow—you can't imagine how—everything will be alright.

Despite the anguish of your heart and the number of times and tears you've cried, your Father knows your sorrow and wants to draw you close to Himself. He will not abandon you. Accept the assurance of God's love and expect His supernatural presence to reveal His messages for you, and over time you will find yourself trusting Him more and more, still unable to explain why difficult things have happened but utterly convinced that God is bigger than any of them.

RESTORE AND RENEW

1. How has God communicated with you in the midst of your suffering? What message has He consistently sent you?
2. What supernatural evidence have you encountered that reveals God's hand at work in your healing? What has surprised or startled you the most?
3. How has God used other people to confirm His presence to you in your healing and restoration?
4. When have you sensed God communicating to you through your dreams? What was the message He gave you? How did He confirm the message in other ways?
5. Where have you seen seeds of hope and new growth appear amidst the ashes of your loss? How is God redeeming your suffering into something precious for His kingdom?

RECONNECT AND REVIVE

Dear God, I know that You're with me and that You're doing a good work in my life. I can't always see what You're up to, but I trust that You will continue to reveal Yourself and to remind me of Your love, protection and guidance during this season of restoration. Amen.

6

Dare to Dance: Overcoming Your Fear of Falling

As my sons grow older, I'm amused by the way their views of the opposite sex have started to change. You know, from "Yuck, girls!" to "She's just a girl in my class" to "Yeah, she's okay." As I recall from my own brush with such things in middle school, young love is a whole new world with uncertain rules and unknown expectations. "What does she think of me?" "Do I look okay?" "Will she like me?" "What if everyone finds out?" "What if everyone finds out, and she *doesn't* like me?"

Soon my boys will be attending school dances and having the same kinds of questions float through their minds. They will realize how scary it can be to take a chance on asking a girl to dance, on igniting a hopeful spark of connection, on feeling less alone. While the music changes with each generation and things may get a little more complicated with texts, Facebook and Twitter, the steps remain the same. Life does indeed seem to be a dance.

And the dance only gets more intense as we grow up. As we move from childhood to adulthood, the stakes become higher—especially as we encounter events that knock us off our feet. As in the kids' game musical chairs, when the music of life stops, we often discover that we have no place left to sit. With each personal loss, deep disappointment or emotional injury, we find it hard to keep taking risks. Our hearts get broken—once, twice, three times; then, like a frozen lake, the cracks run deeper and shatter into more icy pieces.

Life is simply too painful.

Once we come to this realization, we basically have three choices: We can withdraw from life, putting a wall around our heart and developing a protective mask to present to the world. Or we can keep stepping out, risking our heart to get what we want until we're numb with disappointment and despair over the cruel blows we continue to suffer, becoming a victim of circumstance. Or we can look beyond ourselves and turn to God.

God always has room for us and is more than willing to guide us if we'll let Him. Life will still be scary. Painful events will still occur. But when we surrender our hearts to God, we'll no longer be alone, looking outside ourselves to find fulfillment. We'll realize that we have a Father who loves us and empowers us to start over, who will help us get up when we fall, stand back on our feet and follow Him—that we have a Savior who knows how to mend even the iciest, most shattered of lives, a God who can transform our most devastating losses into love.

And that transformation can happen when we least expect it. At least, it did for me.

New Beginnings

After my amazing first date with Cyd, my thoughts were reeling. I actually felt hopeful for the first time since Debra's death that I might be able to love again. That feeling was totally unexpected, a gift that seemed as if it might be a part of God's plan for me. I still missed my wife; I can't deny that I did. But being able to enjoy a delicious meal and openhearted conversation with Cyd gave me hope. A seed had been growing in the darkness of winter and was now bursting through the spring soil. My cold, dark season of heartache was giving way to the light of my Father's glorious plan.

Fortunately, my attraction to Cyd seemed to be mutual. After our fun-filled evening together, I sent her a thank-you card for having dinner with me. I had initially felt extremely awkward about going on a date after having been married for so long. But Cyd had made it more than easy for us to talk and get reacquainted, and I wanted her to know how much I had appreciated her ability to be herself with me. Impressed, apparently, that I had taken the time to write her a note of thanks, she sounded genuinely happy to hear from me when I'd call her after this. Soon she and I naturally fell into a habit of talking regularly—sometimes for an hour or more—after each of us arrived home from work.

Okay, I might as well confess. In hindsight, I was clearly head over heels for Cyd within two weeks after our dinner at Mac's. But several factors helped me keep my feelings under wraps and not rush anything. Obviously, first on my list was my emotional vulnerability due to my intense season of grief and readjustment to life without Debra. Even though I would be coming up on the one-year anniversary of the accident in just a few weeks, I didn't want to rush into anything just because I was sometimes sad and lonely.

A couple other reasons came to mind. First, I didn't want Cyd to think that my Christian faith was of the "granola" variety—you know, that I was one of those fruits, flakes and nuts! Besides, before I told her how I was feeling, I needed to spend some time before God with these new emotions. Second, when I was growing up, my dad had always told me, "Son, don't ever say 'I love you' to a girl until you've taken the time to get to know her." Very powerful words that had stuck with me.

So instead of discussing my feelings with Cyd or telling her that I loved her, I tried to express my care in a more generic way. At the end of our phone conversations, I would simply say, "I appreciate you." She would giggle and say, "Thank you—goodnight."

How corny is that? "I appreciate you"? Really, that was the best I could come up with? I'm still embarrassed thinking about that. But as I said, I was out of practice and wanted to keep things honest and open between us. And as observant and emotionally aware as Cyd is, I could tell that she was picking up my vibe. And it seemed as if she might be feeling the same way I did.

Yes, I knew how I really felt about her. I just didn't know if I trusted those feelings. Was I just eager to feel good again and so leaping at the chance with Cyd? Or was this really God leading me into a new season of my life?

Waiting for a Word

Sometimes when we're undergoing restoration, we can be tempted to rely on our emotions as our only compass for how to proceed. It can be so painful and emotionally debilitating when we're grieving or coming out of a crisis. On one hand, we simply want to feel anything besides the aching hurt that's been inside us for so long. Yet on the other, we're afraid to trust our new feelings. After all, isn't that what happened to us in the first place? Things were going well, we felt good about our life, and then *BAM!*—out of nowhere we were brought to our knees.

Yes, it can be hard to trust our feelings even when they're positive, pleasant and life affirming. So we often hold back, waiting for the other shoe to drop. Maybe this is an attempt at controlling what is ultimately uncontrollable in our lives. Or perhaps we're simply trying to protect ourselves from being blindsided again. Either way, there's a more reliable source of direction than simply what we're feeling.

The Bible tells us that God remains the same yesterday, today and tomorrow. He's described as the great I AM, timeless and eternal, sovereign and all-knowing. There is no change or shifting with God. We can count on Him to be there for us, no matter what we're going through. Whether we have a good day or a bad day does not have to depend on our mood or our emotional response to circumstances. We can turn to Him.

So that's what Cyd and I did. By the first part of November, things between us were getting serious in my mind. Not only were we talking almost every day on the phone, but also at the end of October, Cyd had attended an event at my church.

Not long after that, we finally came clean with each other about where we stood. Clearly, we felt an attraction to one another. But we both agreed that our relationship had to be built on more than romantic feelings. Ultimately, both Cyd and I wanted to hear from God about the future of our relationship. In fact, I had already set a time limit and informed Cyd that I was giving the Lord until December 31 to reveal to me whether she was to be my wife. If I didn't get a clear word, we would not maintain our relationship.

While I didn't want my statement to sound like an ultimatum, I wanted to be clear with her that I could only proceed with a clear sign of God's blessing on us as a couple. I was a little nervous about how Cyd would respond to my words, but without flinching, she said, "I'm 33 years old and have never been married, so I'm not interested in making a mistake now. If you're not to be my husband, I'm asking the Lord to remove you from my life."

Wow! She was the real deal; her relationship with God was clearly just as important to her as mine was to me. I was impressed.

Answering the Call

Thanksgiving was fast approaching, and neither of us had heard a word from the Lord regarding the future of our relationship. During the week of Thanksgiving, I had planned to visit my oldest sister, Jackie, in North Carolina. Cyd and I decided that we would not talk at all that week while I was out of town. We thought it would be good for us to have some time apart. And I certainly didn't want my sister to know I might be serious about someone— she would be like a rooster crowing at dawn with that news!

However, I did give Cyd the phone number of the place where I would be staying in case of an emergency (wink, wink). Needless to say, we did not keep our commitment not to speak with each other. As I remember it, Cyd was not only the first one to place the call but it was also her first time ever to call me. My heart almost jumped out of my chest when I heard her voice on the phone. We had not spoken for three very long days, and it was then, while I was in North Carolina, that I realized that I didn't want to live my life without Cyd. I didn't have a word from the Lord, but this realization was definitely more than a feeling. It was bigger than just my attraction to her.

So the day after Thanksgiving, without really planning ahead, I finally spoke those three little words to her as we concluded our phone call.

"Could you repeat that please?" Cyd asked me.

"I love you," I told her again.

She later revealed to me that she had suspected that I loved her every time I'd said "I appreciate you." My emotions were all over the map at that moment; I was embarrassed, jubilant, giddy, hopeful and bold. There was just one hurdle to jump: the Lord had not said anything about Cyd being my wife. We were getting closer and closer to our self-imposed deadline of receiving a word from Him regarding our relationship. Surely He wouldn't have brought us together if He didn't intend for us to marry, right?

Making Introductions

Sometimes when we wait on the Lord and try to discern His will for our lives, we mistakenly think that His guidance has to be written in the sky or booming in our ears. While I do believe that God speaks to our hearts, I've also found that He often reveals Himself through His people. In other words, men and women who know the Lord often provide us with credible and reliable input on the direction we should take in order to follow the Lord.

Sometimes when we're rebuilding our lives and allowing God to restore our souls, we feel so alone with our pain that we don't even allow others around us. However, as restoration continues, God often brings people into our lives who can help us recover, heal and grow. Many dear friends in my church family had supported me through my grief. Now it seemed like a good idea to see how they would respond to this new direction my life was taking.

As my relationship with Cyd continued to grow deeper, I recognized that it was time for my friends to meet her and for her to meet them. In fact, I had established in my mind that if any of these special friends of mine had serious concerns about her, then I would likely end our relationship. Out of fairness to her, I told this to Cyd. She calmly took it in stride and once again said, "I don't have anything to hide, and if the Lord is in this, He will reveal what needs to be revealed." Therefore, Cyd's first formal introduction to a big group of my friends was at a gathering of the elders and pastors of Covenant Church.

After Cyd's and my conversation, I decided to host a Christmas party at my home to introduce Cyd to the leadership team from my church. During the course of that evening, she was questioned and observed by over 14 different couples. I'm sure that she must have felt like a sacrificial lamb being inspected through and through to see if it qualified as an acceptable offering to the Lord. Before the party I had asked everyone who attended to look for any red flags that might potentially disqualify Cyd as a wife and ministry partner for me.

There was nothing to worry about. By the end of the evening, everyone felt as if they'd known Cyd for years, and they absolutely loved her. One of my fellow pastors stated, "When I talked with her, she maintained steady eye contact, and looking into her eyes, I saw nothing but purity and honesty." Again Cyd made an impact on me. Under tremendous pressure in a room full of strangers, she didn't feel the need to impress anyone or try to be anything other than herself. She clearly knew who she was.

However, one very important couple, Pastors Mike and Kathy Hayes, was not present that night. Their opinions would ultimately carry more weight than those of the others. So Cyd and I arranged for her to meet them at a Christmas concert featuring BeBe Winans.

That night as Cyd and I drove into the parking lot of Covenant Church, nervous energy filled the atmosphere. In just a few minutes she was going to meet my spiritual parents, mentors and employers for the first time. It would also be her first time to be seen with me publicly at a Covenant Church event. Pastor Kathy had instructed me to meet her and Pastor Mike in Apostles Hall.

As we stepped into the elevator, I encouraged Cyd to relax and just be herself. She knew that this was a huge moment for both of us. For more than eight years, members of Covenant Church had only seen one woman walking beside me. And now, barely a few days before the first anniversary of Debra's death, I had brought someone new, a different woman, for them to meet.

As the big double doors to Apostles Hall opened, Cyd and I stepped over the threshold. The noise of the crowd began to soften, and almost with perfect timing a channel opened for us through the crowd of people. Standing at the end of this pathway were Pastors Mike and Kathy.

They had spotted us the moment we walked into the room. Both intently observed Cyd and did not waver from their focus. The distance between us and them was only 10 or 15 feet, but the walk seemed to last an eternity. As we approached them, words from a conversation between Pastor Kathy and me some weeks prior rang out in my mind. She had lovingly told me, "You know, if you get married again, your wife will have to be pastor material."

As we got closer, the Hayeses began to smile. I made the introductions, and we all embraced, knowing that the entire room was watching and buzzing with questions. "Who's that with Pastor Ricky?" "Where did she come from?" "Is that his sister?" Pastor Kathy, with her wonderful gift of hospitality, was very kind as she drew Cyd right in.

Pastors Mike and Kathy invited us to share the evening with them. What an honor it was as we joined them in visiting with BeBe in the green room prior to the concert and later sat with them during his concert. Cyd later shared with me how Pastor Kathy had studied her the entire evening. Whenever Cyd stole a glance her way, she found Pastor Kathy steadily watching her. Sometimes Pastor Kathy wouldn't look away but only smile.

We both had a wonderful time that night and Cyd seemed to fit right in. BeBe moved the crowd with his inspirational singing; the joyous atmosphere created a great mood for celebrating. As I participated in the concert and scanned the audience throughout the evening, I gave thanks to God for the people who had encouraged me, and especially for Cyd standing by my side. Finally, at the end of the evening, I received my pastors' feedback: Pastors Mike and Kathy expressed how lovely Cyd was and how they enjoyed being with us for the evening. They really liked Cyd and could tell that she was a very sharp young lady.

I couldn't agree more. In my mind Cyd had passed the two major hurdles within my Covenant Church family.

Over the course of several weeks, Cyd met other family and friends who were particularly important in my life. There were only two people left for Cyd to meet, and their opinion carried the greatest weight of all: my parents, Robert and Dorothy Texada. I would be going home to Louisiana for Christmas, and since Cyd's mom lived only an hour from my parents, I extended an invitation to Cyd to join me on the drive to our home state and to meet my mom and dad.

I did my best to prepare Cyd for the meeting with my parents. I explained to her that it would be an emotional encounter for a couple reasons: first, we were approaching the one-year anniversary of Debra's death, and second, Debra had been a part of the Texada family for 15 years and had truly been like a daughter to my parents.

My mom had given birth to six sons, and she was fiercely protective of each one of us. In fact, she was known to have run off a few of our girlfriends back in the day. Because of this, I told Cyd that my mom would be nice to her but that she shouldn't expect much else. My dad, however, was a completely different story. Although he would still be grieving our loss of Debra, Dad would understand my desire to move forward. If he thought that Cyd was a good Christian woman, beautiful both inside and out, and if he could see that I was happy with her, he would not hold back his approval.

While all the bases—except for Cyd meeting my parents—had been covered on my side, I still had no clear sense of what the Lord intended for Cyd and me. According to the end-of-year time-frame we had both agreed on, time was running out. Were we missing something? Or was it possible that we were not meant to be together?

Mary Christmas

On the one-year anniversary of Debra's funeral, I woke up and lay in bed in the quiet of my house, going over all that had happened in the span of a year. That terrible, unexpected car accident. The hospital and losing her. Burying Debra in her hometown, where 40 people had given their hearts to the Lord at her funeral service.

As I dressed for church, I cried and thanked the Lord for His goodness to me. A year ago I had felt hopeless, blinded and lost. My world had been turned upside down, and I hadn't known what the future held, nor had I cared—at least at first. I'd had no way of knowing if I would even survive the fateful hand dealt me.

Now there was hope. The Lord had remained present with me throughout my grief and loneliness. I had drawn so much closer to Him, worshiping and praising Him through music, in prayer and by fasting. God had transformed my life, and now I was an ordained minister, and this wonderful young lady named Cyd had walked into my life. So many wonderful things had been revealed to me by my heavenly Father. So my request that day was simple: "Lord, will You just speak to me and let me know if Cyd is to be my wife?"

The worship in our service that morning was exuberant and moving. The Lord, as He had done in times past on significant dates for me, was very near. I could sense His presence in an intimate way, and I knew that He was up to something. Pastor Mike's message, "How to Have a 'Mary' Christmas," described the meeting between Mary, the mother of Jesus, and Elizabeth, the mother of John the Baptist. Scripture indicates that when Elizabeth heard Mary's salutation, John leaped in his mother's womb. Pastor Mike declared, "That's how it is when two lives and their destinies are intertwined; when they come together, there is a divine spark."

When he said this, I felt God's Spirit remind me of a hot summer's day only a few months earlier. I remembered my friend Keith running toward me in the parking lot, handing me a CD and asking me if I'd ever heard of the artist on the cover. Without a doubt I suddenly knew that in that moment a divine spark had ignited the dry tinder of my heart. When I saw Cyd's face on that CD case, even then I knew that something special had just started. Without even knowing her story or where she was at that point, something had come to life in me.

Tears began to stream down my face. God's voice echoed clearly in my heart. I had my answer and wanted to break into Mary's song:

My soul magnifies the Lord, and my spirit has rejoiced in God my Savior. For He has regarded the lowly state of His servant; for behold, henceforth all generations will call me blessed. For He who is mighty has done great things for me, and holy is His name. And His mercy is on those who fear Him from generation to generation. He has shown strength with His arm; He has scattered the proud in the imagination of their hearts. He has put down the mighty from their thrones, and exalted the lowly. He has filled the hungry with good things, and the rich He has sent away empty. He has helped His servant Israel, in remembrance of His mercy, as He spoke to our fathers, to Abraham and to his seed forever (Luke 1:46-55, *NKJV*).

The only thing I had to do now was determine the right time to tell Cyd what God had shown me, because I didn't want to say anything to her until she too had received her confirmation from the Lord.

Listening for the Lord

When she was growing up, Cyd had a wonderful mom who worked really hard, but she didn't know who her dad was. She had one older sister who lived with relatives in another state, and the two girls only saw each other during the summer. So during the school year Cyd was a lonely little girl. She noticed families that had a mom, a dad and sisters and brothers, and they all seemed to have so much fun together. She knew other little girls who had dads who seemed to adore them and who took them places. How she longed for that.

Left to imagine what her father would be like, Cyd dreamed of a warm, kind man who would love her and treat her like a princess. When she was almost 10, her mother finally decided that she was old enough to find out who her daddy was. Her mom began to tell her that he was a man she already knew, a family friend whom Cyd had called Santa Claus because of a beautiful little organ he had given her one year for Christmas. Cyd loved to play that little organ, and she was delighted to find that this nice man was actually her father.

But then the other shoe dropped, because her mom went on to tell Cyd that her daddy couldn't visit that much because he had another family. He was married and had other children, a son and two daughters. Disappointed, Cyd nonetheless held on to her dream and looked forward to the time when she would see "Santa Claus" now that she knew the truth.

When he finally came to visit a few weeks later, Cyd rushed to the door and smiled up at him with great hope and expectancy. But her father's response confused her; he looked at her no differently than usual, mumbled hello and immediately began to visit with her mom.

Needless to say, Cyd's heart was crushed. And it continued to happen over and over again as she pursued his love only to have him make promises that they would spend time together—never to keep a single one of them. She grew up believing that her dad didn't really want her, and if her own dad couldn't love her, how could anyone else? Cyd was convinced that she was a mistake since her parents weren't married and her mom had just happened to get pregnant with her.

When she went off to college, she had an encounter with someone who introduced her to the concept of giving her heart to Jesus. She had grown up in a traditional Baptist Church but had never been told about the opportunity to have a personal relationship with God by accepting the gift that Jesus offered. Once she did this, everything changed in the way she saw life. She knew without a doubt that she wasn't a mistake but that God had specifically created her for a purpose.

By the time I renewed my friendship with her, Cyd had a good relationship with her father and had experienced considerable healing in her heart. She dated from time to time, and while she longed to marry and have a loving family like the one she had once dreamed about, she had not met "the one." So she focused on her relationship with the Lord, dedicated herself to serving Him at her church, and concentrated on advancing her engineering career.

As beautiful as she is, Cyd always had guys flirting with her or trying out their moves on her, but she would have none of it. She wanted a man who was as serious about his relationship with God as she was with hers. The guys she dated were smart and respectful, and several of them had a strong faith, but she never had a sense that any of these relationships would lead to marriage. So she had waited on the Lord to reveal to her the man who would be her husband. And while her feelings for me were just as strong as mine for her, Cyd knew that after waiting so many years for God to answer her prayer, she wasn't going to rely on her feelings alone. She wanted confirmation about our future as much as I did.

A couple days after my "Mary Christmas" revelation, Cyd began her day much like any other: on her knees before the Lord. Feeling the pressure of the looming self-imposed deadline to receive God's yea or nay on our relationship, she whispered, "Oh Father, please tell me something: I need to know if Ricky is supposed to be my husband." She listened patiently for a few minutes and then thought, *If only the phone would ring or something*.

It did. At that moment the phone rang, much to Cyd's amazement. After all, who would be calling her at six in the morning?

"Hello," she answered.

"I'll only visit you on Tuesday," said a woman's voice.

"What? Who is this?" Cyd demanded.

"I'll only visit you on Tuesday," repeated the caller.

"What are you talking about? You must have the wrong—"

"It's Stephanie—your sister! I said that I'll only be able to visit you on Tuesdays when you marry Ricky and move to Carrollton. Danielle has dance lessons in that direction on Tuesdays."

Relieved but still a bit shaken, Cyd said, "Steph, what makes you say that? Why do you think—never mind. Hey, I'm actually praying right now, so can I call you back a little later?"

They exchanged good-byes, but as Cyd hung up her phone, her mind was spinning. "Was that You, Lord? It sure was unusual. Was that the confirmation I've been waiting on?"

It sure seemed like it, because she hadn't had a chance to tell Stephanie how serious things were becoming between us. As she replayed the short conversation in her thoughts, Cyd smiled and believed that she had heard from the Lord. One more experience to come would seal the deal for her.

When she called to tell me what had happened, I shared with her what had occurred with me on Sunday in church. Knowing what we both now knew, our trip home to Louisiana for Christmas took on an entirely new meaning. We wouldn't just be meeting each other's respective families—we would be meeting our future in-laws.

I must admit that I harbored concerns that those who had not witnessed my transformation process during the eight months after Debra's death would think that I was moving too quickly with Cyd. My only consolation rested in the fact that I had not initiated any of the events that had unfolded over the last two and a half months. Yes, it was hard to believe that so much could happen within one year. But I had no doubt whatsoever about God's timing.

Just a year ago, my world had crumbled, my vision had been blinded, and all hope had seemed lost. Now I was driving home to Louisiana with a young lady who had captured my heart and amplified my confidence and trust that the Lord really does have a plan that He works to perfection. There was no other way I could see it.

I just hoped our families would feel the same way.

Meet the Parents

When we arrived at Cyd's mom's house in Opelousas, Louisiana, her mom, Eula Mae Dell, greeted us at the front door. Cyd had warned me that her mom was a little eccentric about cleanliness. "Make sure you wipe your feet before you enter the house; and sit down on the sofa that has a covering over it, because she doesn't want to get things dirty." She also told me, "Always, always wash your hands before you open the refrigerator door."

Despite being nervous, I decided to be myself, and I leaned down to give Cyd's mom a big hug. She warmly hugged me right back as Cyd proudly exclaimed, "Mom, this is Ricky, the guy I've been telling you about."

Ms. Eula had small eyes that seemed to dance as she talked. Her skin tone, a creamy golden hue, was typical of many black South Louisiana women whose ancestry includes French and other European blood. She was dressed in a classy conservative manner and spoke with a soft voice.

In the little time that I had to spend with her before driving to my parents' house near Alexandria, I could tell that she was a spiritually devout woman who loved and was proud of her daughter Cyd. I was also pleasantly surprised to see that Ms. Eula had a good sense of humor. After Cyd jokingly referenced something having to do with flatulence, her mother replied, "You better be careful, or you might run Ricky off!" and then laughed from deep within her belly. I knew right then that I really liked her.

I left Cyd with her mom and headed to my parents' home. After a couple days apart, I went back to pick up Cyd on Christmas day as planned and brought her to meet my parents at their home. My mom and dad live about eight miles west of Alexandria on a small picturesque homestead that's been in the Texada family since 1903. Their wood-framed white house with black shutters sits on a small hill facing west with two magnificent pecan trees rising out of the ground at the corners of their yard.

As I ushered Cyd into the house, Mom greeted her with a friendly smile and a warm hug. As I turned to go outside to get my dad, he was already coming toward me from his toolshed. His first words to me were, "Ricky, she's gorgeous! She's beautiful! You gonna marry her?" I laughed out loud and said casually, "I might."

We had a great day as Cyd met different members of the family. A steady stream of people, including my Aunt Madea (yes, most families had one long before Tyler Perry!), came to the house with Christmas greetings. Cyd was her usual self—friendly, dynamic and full of life.

Cyd would later share with me that the cry of her heart had always been to be part of a family in which the mom and the dad were married and committed to each other. After watching my family, including my siblings, their spouses and their children, she felt as if she had found the place she belonged, and she believed that this was God's answer to the prayer of her heart. Now she truly believed that God had confirmed the future of our relationship.

When our time with the family started to wind down, I prepared to take Cyd back to Opelousas. I invited Mom and Dad to join us for the one-hour drive. The drive to Cyd's hometown was filled with conversation about everything from Cyd's family to her plans when she arrived back in Dallas. Once at Ms. Eula's house, we spent a little time allowing our parents to converse. I genuinely felt good about the day.

As we got on the interstate for our drive back to Alexandria, I said to my parents, "Well—what do you think?"

My mom simply said, "She fits."

My dad exclaimed, "I was just about to say the same thing!"

"Mom, what do you mean?" I asked, although I had a pretty good idea.

She thought for a moment. "Even though today was the first day that I met her, it seems as if she has always been part of our family."

"I agree," my dad replied.

I knew then, beyond a shadow of a doubt, that I was going to ask Cyd to marry me. The question now was when, where and how?

Start the Music

Once God has revealed Himself and provided direction for us, then we must take action. Too often I fear that we want the process of restoration to be instantaneous and comprehensive. But this isn't the way it usually works. It takes time and is a process. In fact,

I'm convinced that the process—made up of the small steps of faith that we take along the way—is often how we are restored.

God had spoken and consistently confirmed His message to us—through other people, through my Mary Christmas moment and through Stephanie's call to Cyd. With no doubt about my love for her and God's desire for us to be married, I realized what my next step should be.

So before going back to Dallas, I asked Cyd's mom for her daughter's hand in marriage. Cyd was dropping off a Christmas present at her cousin's house, so I took the opportunity to seek my future mother-in-law's blessing. Ms. Eula chuckled and said, "Are you sure you want to marry her?"

"Without a doubt," I said.

As she wiped tears from her eyes, she said, "Well, okay then!"

Cyd didn't know what I had done. Later that afternoon I placed a call to her dad, presenting the question to him as well. In his deep baritone voice, he replied, "Sure, that's wonderful. Thanks for asking me."

All that was left now was my proposal to Cyd. I could hardly wait until we got back to Dallas. I felt pretty confident as to what her response would be. And I was grateful in ways that I had never been grateful before. God's goodness had never tasted sweeter.

I wonder sometimes if we only appreciate just how good God is by suffering through what we've lost. Not that God takes people or things away from us if we're not adequately grateful—just the contrary. I think that one of the ways the Lord redeems our losses is to help us appreciate what we had, to grieve it and then to risk more by loving again. When we've lost something and then been blessed to have the Lord restore that area in our lives, we can't help but be even more filled with gratitude.

As we experience restoration in our lives, the dance may not go as smoothly as we would like. The music might stop before it starts again. We might step on a few toes or have others step on ours. We might make a few awkward mistakes and temporarily lose our balance or rhythm. But ultimately, no matter how wounded we've been, we dare to dance again.

If you're struggling with how to move forward, I encourage you to notice the blessings presently in your life even as you continue trusting God with your future. It won't be easy—you'll still be tempted to sit out the dance—but our Father's promises are more powerful than all our pain put together. He *will* restore us if we let Him.

Can you hear the music? I think it's your song. Take a deep breath and take the first step. That's all He asks you to do.

RESTORE AND RENEW

1. How would you describe the present tempo of your life? Are you moving more slowly than usual, or do you feel pulled in every direction at warp speed?
2. What's the new direction you sense God calling you to pursue? What risk is He asking you to take today?
3. What new relationships or opportunities for new relationships have emerged in your life in the past few weeks? How have you responded to these opportunities to get to know new people?
4. How have you responded to God's gifts and blessings lately? Have you accepted them reluctantly? Wholeheartedly? Or have you ignored them altogether?
5. When was the last time you felt your heart grow lighter or perhaps even allowed a moment of joy or hope?

RECONNECT AND REVIVE

Lord, I know that You're at work in my life—I can't deny the evidence of Your blessings. Thank You for all You give me and for the seeds of new life that are beginning to sprout before my very eyes. Amen.

7

Open the Present:
Learning to Say Yes Again

Like most children, my sons love to unwrap presents. Or let me say it more accurately: they love to get to what's *inside* the present! They rip through shiny foil paper under the tree on Christmas morning faster than Cyd or I can say, "Who's that from?" And on their birthdays it's all we can do to get the candles lit and blown out on the cake before they're tearing into the brightly colored gifts from family and friends. And after all, who can blame them? Unless we already know what's inside, we all love to discover what's hidden beneath the wrapping paper.

Well, maybe not everyone. On the opposite end of the spectrum would be ladies like my mother-in-law, who not only takes her sweet time opening a present carefully so that the pretty paper and ribbon can be recycled but also seems to savor the thought and effort that went into the wrapping of the present. How impatient all of us get waiting on her to open her Christmas presents at our family holiday times. She seems to take about 10 minutes per package, but I'm sure it's more like 30 seconds compared to the 2 it takes us.

As I've gotten older, I've realized that the sense of anticipation and excitement that we had opening presents as children has disappeared. Whether we rush and rip the package open or take our time and appreciate the beautiful wrapping, we usually don't expect to be surprised. It's probably going to be the tie we asked for or the new coffee maker that we need, a pretty pair of earrings to match the necklace we already have or an electric screwdriver for the toolkit. It's not that we aren't grateful for these gifts; it's simply that we know what to expect. This keeps us from being either surprised or disappointed.

In our lives, however, we sometimes come to a crossroads at which we find a gift waiting to be unwrapped. We may know that it's from God and that therefore it's a good gift, since that's the only kind of present our Father bestows on us. However, we may still be reluctant to open the present and accept the gift. When we've lost something precious to us, whether it's a loved one or an opportunity, we're often reluctant to embrace even the good gifts that come our way.

We may be afraid of caring again, or we may worry about the potential for future pain if and when we lose this new present. Maybe we worry about what other people think or how they will perceive us if we accept God's blessing. Will they assume that we're rushing into something just to avoid the painful grief and heartache that we experienced? Will they think that we didn't really care about what we lost?

These are all normal concerns and questions to have during the process of restoration. However, we must never allow our fears, doubts or sorrows to prevent us from moving forward with our lives. Nor can we allow the opinions, perceptions and speculations of other people to dictate the decisions we make. When God offers us a divinely appointed present, we must say yes.

Popping the Question

Taking this step is easier to talk about than to do. Even when it's clear that God is leading and guiding us into a joyful, amazing, better-than-we-could-imagine situation, it can feel scary. Maybe it's the fact that we still feel blindsided by the loss we experienced that causes us to move slowly or even reluctantly: Is this too good to be true? Or perhaps it's simply another kind of test of our trust in God: Is He really for me? Does God really want me to experience joy and peace and restoration? We know the right answer in our heads, but allowing that message into our hearts takes time and does indeed require faith.

Even though I knew that I wanted to marry Cyd and felt 100 percent confident that God had brought us together, I still felt as if I were jumping off a cliff in asking her to marry me. In some ways it would be easier and require less effort if I continued on alone. Others would continue to comfort me, feel sympathy for me and want to take care of me. They wouldn't wonder about whether or not I still loved Debra or whether I was rushing into another relationship too soon.

But in the end it came back to what I knew God wanted me to do.

So after we returned to Dallas from our Christmas visit to Louisiana, I called my good friend Kitty Cochran. A classy lady with brilliant red hair, eyes that twinkled with mischief and a personality to match, Kitty used her keen eye for detail in her work as an interior designer. Since Kitty had never met a stranger, it seemed that she knew practically everyone in the business community, including those who worked at the Dallas Market Hall. Market Hall was the place where vendors from all over the nation came to place merchandise orders for every type of product you can name. After I explained where things were in my relationship with Cyd, Kitty agreed to show me the perfect jeweler at Market Hall from whom I could purchase the wedding rings.

Cyd obviously knew that I was going to pop the question sometime in the near future. However, she didn't know what kind of ring I would purchase or when I would ask her to marry me.

I had confided to Kitty that I planned to propose on New Year's Day. Because Cyd wanted a trillion cut diamond, Kitty and I found a stone that the jeweler had planned to use as an earring stud and had it mounted on a wedding band. Set in a three-prong mounting, the diamond rested on a platinum band that was simple but elegant. Without Cyd's knowledge I arranged to pick the ring up on New Year's Eve.

That evening, Cyd and I dressed in our Sunday best to have dinner at Antares Restaurant, located at the top of Reunion Tower in downtown Dallas. This restaurant, 48 stories high and built on a rotating platform, offered a panoramic view of the Dallas skyline. It took one hour to complete one full rotation. The dining consisted of a four-course meal: appetizers, salads, entrees and dessert.

We enjoyed our meal and reminisced about our recent visit back home in Louisiana, happily relaxed and at ease with one another. As we completed our delicious entrees, I asked Cyd if she was ready for dessert, knowing full well what was about to happen. She didn't have a clue that I had instructed the waiter to bring out a bed of chocolate-covered strawberries on a serving platter. In the middle of the strawberry display would be a small covered serving dish. The box with the ring would be inside the covered dish.

By this time word had spread among the wait staff that a proposal was about to be made. The energy and tension in the restaurant were palpable. As servers and bussers passed by our table, they would acknowledge me with a discreet smile or wink. When the waiter arrived with the dessert tray, Cyd and I continued exchanging small talk. As the platter was placed in front of her, Cyd made an expression that puzzled me, so I asked her if something was wrong. She replied, "I'm going to let you eat those. I'm pretty full right now."

A year later it would be brought to my attention that Cyd didn't even like strawberries.

Okay, I'd better come up with Plan B, I remember thinking. So we continued talking as I downed a couple of the strawberries. I began to tell her what joy she had brought back into my life and the difference that she had made over the last couple months since our first meeting with each other. I went on to tell her that I had received permission from her mom and dad to ask for her hand in marriage. She was surprised and wanted to know when I'd had time to speak to them.

Continuing our conversation, I told Cyd that I was prepared to spend the rest of my life with her. As I said that, I raised the cover of the small platter, exposing the little black ring box. Opening the box and exposing the triangular-shaped diamond, I slid out of my chair, moved to her side of the table, fell to my left knee and said, "Cyd, will you marry me?"

She began to cry and fanned her face. She was so elated that she immediately picked up her cell phone to call her mom. "Mom, Ricky just asked me to marry him!" She began to describe to her mother the setting that we were in, what we had eaten for dinner and how the ring had come out on a platter full of chocolate-covered strawberries. Meanwhile, I still had not heard the magic word. While still on bended knee, I let her chat for a few moments and then intervened. "Cyd, you didn't give me an answer . . ."

"*Yes!*" she replied with a sheepish grin.

Everyone near our dining table, along with the restaurant staff, erupted into a resounding cheer and began clapping their hands. We kissed and basked in the warmth of the moment. It was simply beautiful.

Now the real work was about to begin.

Questions had to be answered about the wedding date, the wedding, Cyd's career, living arrangements. . . on and on. She and I began to talk about all the transitions she was about to face: walking away from her career of over 10 years as an engineer to rely solely upon my provision for her, leaving her church of many years to get married and become a pastor's wife, and moving to a new city.

When would she transition to Covenant Church? She was currently serving as the assistant worship leader at her church. Was she ready to be a pastor's wife? How would she handle in a few short months five major life changes all at once? All we could do now was what we had done up to now: trust God! Again, it sounds easy now—after all, we loved each other and knew that God had brought us into each other's lives—but we still had challenges to face.

The day following our official engagement I spent making calls to family and to my closest friends. It was amazing to think that just over one year ago, I had been in the throes of despair, and now I was soaring like an eagle on a breezy spring day. God had proven His faithfulness throughout this entire ordeal; my trust in Him was more deeply entrenched than ever. I offered exuberant thanksgiving to Him over and over and over again while everyone rejoiced in receiving our good news.

Cyd's and my engagement was not just my testimony of how God had proven Himself faithful in delivering me, but it was Cyd's testimony as well. Her colleagues at work had thought that she would become an old maid in light of the fact that all she did was work and attend church. Her Christian friends had felt that her standards were too high and that the man she'd been looking for simply didn't exist. Now the Lord was rewarding her faithfulness as well.

Within a day or so, Cyd and I chose April 11 as our wedding date without realizing that it was also Easter weekend. Once we saw this on the calendar, it actually seemed prophetic. It felt as though the Father had resurrected me from the dead by restoring life to me through reviving my hopes of serving with my wife in ministry and of one day becoming a father.

Just Say Yes

Life would be like a whirlwind for Cyd and me over the next several months as she began the transition into her five major life changes. More than ever I trusted God at a level I had not previously experienced. The first two months after Debra's death had been like starting life completely over. Not only because I was single again but also because I was compelled to draw closer to this great God. Even though He had allowed such a tragedy to occur in my life, I still trusted Him.

My spiritual rebirth had happened when I was 18. After that my spiritual journey had been elevated to a whole new level. My salvation experience, coupled with the basic spiritual foundation given me by my parents, had allowed me to endure some difficult days throughout the years. However, none of those days could compare to ones I had experienced on my journey over the past year.

Often people ask me how I managed to get through that season of grief after the devastating accident that forever changed my life. How I maintained my sanity and faith can only be answered with the statement, "I trusted God." Sure, I had trusted Him during the most difficult season of my life, but now, with a new wife-to-be, I realized that my ability to trust the Lord had derived its source from Him and Him alone. He had given me everything I needed to survive and thrive. I knew that the only way to keep moving forward was to keep saying yes to God.

God's fundamental question "Will you trust Me?" remains the same for all of us. Especially when we're going through a season of restoration, we must remember that all we have to do is say, "Yes, Lord." It won't be easy, and it will definitely require more from us than we feel capable of giving. But because we are empowered by Him, we will always be given what we need at the time we need it.

As I anticipated the season of engagement that Cyd and I had just embarked upon, I didn't know whether the waters would be smooth (as they appeared to be) or stormy (as I knew they could always become). Though I shuddered to think that something more tragic could happen to me than that which had occurred on December 17 a little more than a year before, an unshakable trust had been embedded within me. Now, in these next four months, the next chapter of this journey would begin.

And it wouldn't always be smooth sailing.

At the Altar

April 11 finally arrived. I had not slept much the night before as I tossed and turned in anticipation of this big day. I got up very early. In my morning prayer time, all I could do was thank the Lord for His favor and blessing. Again, I was overwhelmed at how God, in His infinite mercy and foreknowledge, had crafted a plan for my life that would give hope to many others during their own difficult days.

Today I would make a covenant with a young lady whom I had initially met 16 years earlier when I was a sophomore and she was a freshman in college. I still couldn't believe that I was getting married to Cyd Patton. During our college years we had been acquainted with each other, and we'd had mutual friends, but we hadn't fraternized in the same circles. I still marveled that this day had been no mystery to my heavenly Father. He'd had a plan from the very beginning, and though phases of that plan had brought me great pain, the big picture was unfolding beautifully like the fresh new Easter lilies on this spring morning.

Because of the relationship that Pastors Mike and Kathy had with Trinity Broadcasting Network (TBN) owners Paul and Jan Crouch, our wedding was being held at the TBN studios in Irving, Texas, on TBN's international television set. It was only the second time in TBN's history that permission had been granted to host a wedding in the studio. The Crouches had heard about the tragedy-to-triumph story of God's redemption in my life and were delighted to bless us.

Cyd was 33 and had waited for the right man; her day had finally arrived. Because of the number of people who had stood by her for so many years, we had a large wedding party—eight brides-maids and eight groomsmen, to be exact. As I gathered with the men—Gordon Banks, Twain Texada, Reggie Texada, Keith Craft, Mike England, Angelo Reid, Shawn Atkinson and Jerry Parsons—my mind reverted to the biblical story of Abraham and Isaac.

God had promised a son to Abraham when the patriarch was 75 years old—a promise that seemed to become more and more impossible considering Abraham's wife Sarah's advanced age as well. But when Abraham was almost 100 years old, his son Isaac was born. But their story didn't end there. Some years later God told Abraham to offer his only son as a sacrifice (see Gen. 22). Abraham's love for God and his faith that God had a plan and would keep His promise—"I will make you a father of many nations" (see Gen. 17:4)—caused him to obey. He said yes to God. It may sound crazy to us, but because of our limited, earth-bound vision, many things that sound unbelievable to us are clearly in God's perfect plan. If someone had told me that I would be marrying again within 16 months of losing Debra, I would never have believed it. And yet God clearly had a plan and had asked me to trust Him, just as He asked Abraham to trust Him with Isaac.

Many biblical scholars believe that Isaac was 33 at the time Abraham offered him to the Lord. Obviously Isaac was younger and stronger than his father, who had to have been around 133 at the time. Isaac could easily have fought his father and dismissed his father's attempt to sacrifice him as the product of senility. He could have lovingly defended himself and prevented his father from carrying out what seemed to him like an irrational, even crazy, plan. But Isaac also said yes to God by submitting to his father.

Isaac trusted his father and knew that his father loved him. Isaac had heard the story time and time again about how long his parents had trusted God and waited... and waited... and waited for him to be born. Isaac knew how precious he was to them, a living testimony to God's faithfulness. He knew that his father would not risk his son's life if doing so were not from God; in fact, God was the only One for whom Abraham would have made such a sacrifice.

And we know the rest of the story. After Abraham said yes by his willingness to sacrifice what he treasured most, God provided him with a ram in the thicket to sacrifice, and Isaac's life was spared.

Some time after this event took place, Abraham said to his chief servant, "Go and find a bride for my son, a bride from my own nation and my own people" (see Gen. 24:1-4). When we consider this story against the life of Christ, we see how the types in this story foreshadowed God giving His own Son, Jesus, who actually *was* sacrificed for mankind, after which the Father God began to prepare a bride (the church) for Him.

As I stood at a different kind of altar on my wedding day, about to join the rest of my life with Cyd's, I felt a kinship with Isaac. As a son, I had submitted to the Father's will; I had not struggled to break free of the process that the Lord had allowed but had submitted myself willingly and patiently. After I had passed the test, the Father had said to His servant, my friend Keith Craft, "Go and get a bride for My son. Get someone who is from his nation and his people of Louisiana." Yes, on this day my joy was inexpressible and full of glory. I felt praise and thanksgiving for my Father who had been so merciful to me. The psalmist knew this feeling well, because he wrote, "*The* LORD *is good* and *His mercy endures forever!*" (see Ps. 106:1, emphasis added).

You're a Gift from Above

As we left the room where the groomsmen had dressed, I reminded Pastor Gordon to make sure he had the rings. The walk from this room to the studio where the wedding would be held was about three minutes, and I didn't want anything to go wrong. Gordon assured me with a wink that he had me covered.

When the men and I finally arrived in the studio, a crowd of more than 600 people were already present. The atmosphere was filled with many emotions: the curiosity of those who had only heard about Cyd but had never seen her; joy, because God's plan was powerfully on display; nervousness, because that's just one of the emotions people feel when such an important event occurs; tension, because there are always family dynamics (Jim Bob is wondering what Bobby Ray is doing here); and love. Cyd and I were both loved by our friends and fellow church members, and we had lots of them because of our commitment to the house of the Lord and the vision of our pastors.

Cyd's Pastor, Dr. Jerry Wolcson, served as a joint officiator of the ceremony with my pastor, Pastor Mike Hayes. Dr. Wolcson, whom Cyd affectionately called Pops, became the pastor of the church that Cyd had attended after its founding pastor had retired. Pops and his wife, Teresa, were an awesome couple who had taken Cyd under their wings after they had arrived to pastor the church. They had seen in her what she had not seen in herself and given her ministry opportunity that had created part of the foundation for her role as a pastor's wife. They meant a lot to Cyd, and because they cared so much for her, I loved and respected them.

Just before we took our places, Pastor Mike informed us that he wasn't feeling well and so would allow Dr. Wolcson to conduct most of the ceremony. I tried to give him an escape route to go home, because it was obvious how he was feeling. He's one of my heroes—always has been and always will be. But he refused to leave, I presume, because he knew how important this day was for me.

As the music began, the bridal party started making its entrance. Cyd, with the help of Pastor Kathy and Sheila Craft, Keith's wife, had chosen a soft lavender satin halter gown for her bridesmaids. The men were in black tuxedos with vests and banded collar shirts; I was arrayed in the same. The wedding party came in, each member with a big smile on his or her face. I was smiling so hard that it felt as if my jaws were locked into place. Everyone was now in their positions—it was time for the bride to enter.

Cyd came toward me down a set of stairs that were almost directly to the right of where I was standing. At the bottom of the stairs she made a right turn and walked about 20 feet toward the back of the room before making a left turn that would bring her to the center aisle up which she would walk.

She had chosen a beautiful pearl- and sequin-covered gown. The gown's train seemed about 10 feet long. As she walked, I took note of as much detail as I could. The shades of eye shadow and dark penciled outlines accentuated her big beautiful brown eyes. A small touch of glitter sparkled on her creamy smooth skin as the warm studio lights cast a soft glow on her face.

She was so stunningly beautiful that I found myself breathless; my heart was energetically and joyously beating faster with each step she took toward me. There she was, now standing in the main aisle, looking lovingly at me. Anyone who has ever met Cyd, if he or she remembers nothing else, will remember her gigantic smile and the whitest of teeth perfectly shaped to fit her gorgeous lips. Women have been known to pay thousands of dollars to have lips shaped like Cyd's.

As she began to draw closer to me, I snapped out of the fanciful trance that her beauty had cast upon me. I prayed to myself, *Ohhhhhh my goodness, this is really happening! God, I sure hope that You know what You're doing, because I don't know this girl!* Compared to the amount of time that I had dated my first wife—four and a half years versus six months with Cyd—I really didn't know her. However, what it came down to was that I trusted the Lord. I knew Him. And I also knew Cyd well enough to know that she knew and trusted Him too.

"Who gives this woman to be married to this man?" Dr. Wolcson asked.

"Her mother and I," Cyd's dad replied.

With my heart pounding I stepped toward Cyd, not taking my eyes off her glowing face, gently grabbed her hand and whispered, "I love you."

Then the most touching thing happened as we stood there looking at each other. An announcement was made that the bride wanted a song played that she had written and prerecorded for me. Wow! I couldn't believe it. It was hard to take it all in. The song's title was "You're a Gift from Above":

There are no words I can say to express how I feel right now.

No one can see what you mean to me.
I don't know how I could deserve one like you.

Our lives entwined for His cause. We are prisoners, yet we
   are free.
Jesus has paid our ransom so we
   could be as one as we fulfill His cause.

You're a gift from above; a yielded soldier fighting for the
   Lord, telling the world of His love,
And how I've longed to be your willing partner who could
   clearly see a fulfillment of His love, of His love.

Two hearts that beat as one is how I envisioned His plan.
Jesus has caused our destinies to be joined in His name,
   He has made you and me.

You're a gift from above, a yielded soldier fighting for
   the Lord, telling the world of His love.

And how I've longed to be your willing partner who
   could clearly see.

I can clearly see this is how He envisioned it to be.
Forever, forever, forever.
Forever,
You and me.

Cyd later explained to me that she had started writing this song a couple years before she met me. However, it was not completed until after we started dating. The song was beautiful and very moving. It obviously captured the journey of her heart and her feelings both about me and about her heavenly Father who had brought me to her. It seemed to be one more amazing moment from God, a reminder of the gift that we had each been given. A reminder that yes, we were taking a risk. But to withhold our hearts and refuse the gift would have required us to stop trusting God and to miss out on one of the greatest blessings of our lives.

The Ring of Truth

After the charge was given, it was time for the vows. This was to be one of the proudest and most tender moments of the ceremony, because I had decided to write our vows. Trying my hand at being a poetic maestro, I had penned the words days before the wedding as only a skilled thespian could. It's funny how what I wrote and what Pops had us repeat didn't contain the same magic as they had when I had scripted those words from my heart full of love.

In fact, I was totally embarrassed and thankful that only a handful of people knew I had written the vows, because when we began repeating them, the words went on and on and on and on.

I could hear the thoughts of people: *My goodness, who wrote those vows, and how are they going to remember what they pledged? Or Come on, preacher, we don't have all day. After all, it is Easter weekend.* So much for my attempt to be a poet!

The ring ceremony came next. When Dr. Wolcson asked for the rings, I turned to Gordon to receive them. He put his right hand into the left inside pocket of his tuxedo jacket. With the most puzzled look of disbelief, his eyes told me that he did not have the rings. Dr. Wolcson looked as if he had just seen a ghost. I could feel the blood rising to my head because I had told Gordon to be sure he had the rings. Now it would take at least six minutes for him to go back to the groomsmen's dressing room to retrieve them.

Standing next to Gordon was Keith Craft. I noticed that Gordon had turned to Keith, inquiring as to whether Keith had the ring. Keith searched his pocket, to no avail. The next groomsman was Shawn Atkinson, who searched frantically in his tuxedo pockets. This action repeated itself with each groomsman until the very last one, Mike England. As Mike searched his pockets, he pulled out the little black case that contained our covenant symbols. Everyone gave a huge sigh of relief, which was followed by quiet laughter.

As Dr. Wolcson quit sweating bullets, I looked at Gordon and silently mouthed, "You nearly caused me to have a heart attack!" He smiled and said, "Gotcha!"

Pastor Mike stepped up to perform his part of the ceremony and concluded with the final pronouncement, "I now pronounce you husband and wife. You may now kiss your bride." The moment I had been waiting for. My heart leapt with joy. She belonged to me now: Mrs. Ricky Texada—that had a nice ring to it.

It had been an incredible day, and this phase of God's redemptive plan was completed. I was no longer a widower, and the prophetic words that had been spoken over Cyd regarding the man she would marry had come to pass. (Several years before this event, a friend of Cyd's, whom she respected as a prophetic voice in her life, privately told her that she was going to marry a powerful man of God. The friend further stated that Cyd was being groomed for ministry at a higher level in another place. Her pastor, Dr. Wolcson, publicly confirmed that she would marry a "powerful man" at a later time. It is interesting that my name, "Ricky," means "rich and powerful ruler.")

God had given each of us a present that we could never have imagined.

We'd only had to say yes and keep trusting Him.

You can do the same.

Your Box Is Never Empty

No matter where you are on your journey, and whether you can sense the restorative power of the Lord or not, your story is not over. When Cyd was growing up, struggling with feelings of inferiority and uncertainty because her father was not around, she couldn't imagine that she would one day marry a man who loved her so deeply. When she was dating, watching her friends marry and start families of their own, she could have settled and compromised her heart as well as her faith. But she didn't. She trusted God and waited on Him.

Certainly after I lost my wife, I could easily have locked up my heart and refused to open it to anyone. I could have played the grieving victim of tragedy and wallowed in my sadness until it turned into self-pity and entitlement. I could have been afraid of what it would cost me to risk my heart and to love again. Or I had the option to trust God and what He had for me. To trust Him with *whom* He had for me.

Presents are meant to be accepted, and they're meant to be opened. Once when I was at the mall with my boys at Christmas, we stopped in front of a store window. The display included a beautiful tree with dozens of perfectly wrapped presents beneath it. Seth asked me, "Dad, who are all those presents for?" I smiled and explained that they were empty boxes, just for decoration. He thought for a moment and said, "I'm so glad that the presents I get have good things inside them!"

Seth had inadvertently stumbled onto a piece of great wisdom. Scripture tells us that if we who are flawed and sinful love to give our children good gifts, then how much more does our Father in heaven delight in giving us such presents (see Matt. 7:11). When we trust God, our box is never empty. He is always there for us. Even through the darkest night when nothing makes sense and no one else can comfort us, He remains the same. His love is constant. We only have to say yes to the present that He holds before us.

The timing may surprise us, the messenger may surprise us, and the gift itself may not look the way we expected it to, but when it's from God, we can trust that it's the perfect gift for us. God has a present for you. Maybe you can't see it yet, but it's there, waiting for you. Keep going, my friend—tear through the paper, untie the ribbon, and get to what's waiting inside.

RESTORE AND RENEW

1. What do you feel about the way God brought Cyd into my life? Is it easier for you to relate to my grief over losing Debra or to my joy in discovering God's gift of Cyd to me?
2. When has God surprised you by His timing? How does He continue to interrupt your schedule and your default rhythm with His interventions?
3. How has your attitude toward God changed since you began reading this book?
4. How has the way you process your loss and express your grief changed in the past few days?
5. What keeps you from experiencing the joy of the Lord that He wants to give you today? Are you willing to move out of the way and let go of your grief so that you can embrace the new life God has for you?

RECONNECT AND REVIVE

Heavenly Father, I feel so torn and conflicted sometimes. I'm starting to come alive again, and I see Your many blessings in my life. But I still get scared and wonder if I can trust these new feelings of joy, hope and love. Remind me that You are for my good and that You want to bless me. Amen.

8

Test Your Testimony: Remembering God's Faithfulness

Last fall both of our sons played football in community recreation leagues. Cyd and I had discussed it in advance, and we'd both had reservations—our fear of injury, the extra time that would be required of our family for practices and games, and our boys' potential discouragement at sitting on the bench or even having a losing season. But we also knew that a good coach could teach our boys the value of contributing to a team, the necessity of having a game plan, and the importance of good sportsmanship. We knew how badly they wanted to play. After all, we do live in Texas—the home of the Cowboys, the Texans and *Friday Night Lights*!

While the practices and weekend games made us feel like the boys were in the NFL instead of Pop Warner, I have to say that overall it was a great experience. On different teams according to their ages, both Seth and Caleb enjoyed playing and experienced winning seasons. They had great coaches who interacted well with the boys on their teams. Our boys learned a few lessons about human ego—including their own—and about being part of something bigger than their own abilities. Caleb's team even advanced to the playoffs for its division and ended up in the regional "Super Bowl." They lost that final game, but the thrill of having been there lasted a long time.

During the season Cyd and I frequently took pictures on our phones like most proud parents do. We even printed some of them to post on our fridge and on the kids' bulletin boards. One day at the end of the season, we were going through them together with the boys, and Caleb asked us why we took so many pictures of them running up and down the field. I pointed to one from early in the fall and said, "Well, remember how scared you were at first? Remember how you felt like you didn't know what to do in that first game?"

"Da-ad!" he said, as if I were showing naked baby photos of him to his future wife (that's a few years down the road!).

"What?" I asked innocently and chose another pic. "Here, this was the game when you made that awesome tackle and kept the other team from scoring—remember?"

A big smile lit up his face.

"What about me?" asked Seth. "What did I do?"

So we went through the whole season progressively, commenting on how they'd grown and developed. I explained that someday they would enjoy going through the pictures, remembering all that they'd accomplished that season, and would be amazed at how far they'd come. "When you become the first pair of brothers to win back-to-back Heisman Trophies, I want you to remember what these pictures represent!"

They giggled hysterically as Cyd and I shared a smile and hugged them close.

Even if I was only half teasing, I really want my sons to understand why it's so important for them to track the milestones in their lives. It's not so they can take pride in their own efforts or boast to others. It's simply so they can begin to understand how God works in people's lives. The Lord doesn't necessarily care if they're great football players as long as they're learning lessons that will teach them how to become godly men.

We don't have to play sports or win awards for our achievements to trace the same pattern of God's involvement in our lives. Photographs freeze a moment in time and remind us of special events, important milestones and beautiful scenes that mean something to us. But even more important are the pictures engraved on our hearts and our willingness to commemorate the milestones of God's faithfulness.

Breaking Your Back

We all need reminders of our past triumphs, especially the ones in which we've experienced the protection of the Lord, been blessed by His provision or witnessed the redemptive transformation of a trial into a trophy. And perhaps this last one is the most significant, because it may have the greatest power to remind us of God's faithfulness the next time we encounter an obstacle or receive an injury.

Even after we've experienced healing, we will still suffer other losses in our lives. And surprisingly, these may have fewer consequences but greater impact. We may be so weary and our hearts may feel so fragile that we shrink in fear at something that's really not as harsh as we think it is.

In fact, sometimes in the process of our restoration we reach an impasse. Just as we're starting to hope again, we look up in time to see another crisis looming on the horizon. Something or someone is about to block our path. It might be a relapse of the disease from which we have just recovered. It might be a relational conflict based on someone's response to the changes in our life. Maybe it's an unexpected bill that consumes the remainder of our budget for the month.

Whatever it is, big or small, it feels enormous—the proverbial straw that breaks the camel's back. We're weary and tired, heart sore and scarred from the events we've already faced. We're *done*.

During restoration we may feel so fragile and depleted that we cannot imagine handling one more problem, one more obstacle, one more demand on our lives. We begin to feel as if we can't catch a break, that it's just one bad thing after another. We may even wonder if the Lord has finally abandoned us.

But this is when we need to dig in and go deeper. This is when our faith becomes tested, refined and stronger than we could ever have imagined. This is when the battle turns and we begin to realize that no matter how disappointing or debilitating or devastating our circumstances appear, the Lord remains faithful.

This is when we return to the battlefield and prepare to win the fight, no matter how many times we may have lost before.

This is when we step out in faith, trusting the Lord with a deeper, abiding confidence in His goodness and love.

This is when we raise our Ebenezer.

Back and Forth

Now if you're like me, you may never have heard of an Ebenezer except as the first name of Mr. Scrooge in *A Christmas Carol*. Or if you grew up around church music, you may have heard it in one of my favorite old hymns—more about that in a moment. But the term actually comes from Scripture and refers to a kind of monument that Samuel and God's people erected to mark the place where they defeated their archenemies the Philistines.

Let's set the scene. The people of Israel had basically migrated to Egypt, where their own man Joseph was second in command, in order to survive a terrible famine. Joseph, the dreamer, had been forewarned about the famine and had stored up plenty of grain. So the Israelites stayed in Egypt for a while. A few years down the road, a new pharaoh took the throne, and eventually the Hebrews found themselves enslaved.

Then God raised up Moses to warn the Egyptians and to inflict them with some plagues before leading His people out of Egypt and down the center aisle of the parted Red Sea. Then the Israelites ended up having to wander in the desert for 40 years. Finally they settled in the Promised Land, despite their fickleness toward God. In fact, the people of Israel seem pretty representative of most of us: one day following God and giving thanks to Him for His deliverance and provision, the next day wandering off on our own to find the nearest idol.

For the Israelites it was the foreign gods—and a golden calf that they came up with on their journey. For us it tends to be money, sex, fame, material possessions or an addictive substance. Apparently ever since Adam and Eve blew it in the garden, human nature has tended to relate to God in a push-pull kind of way. We follow Him, we stray, we need help, He delivers us, we follow Him, we stray, back and forth—you get the idea. It's as if we get spiritual amnesia and suddenly forget what God has done for us. And then we get in trouble and remember.

So that's what had happened with the people of Israel as we pick up this scene. Now they were finally trying to turn back to God and follow Him again. But they encountered a major problem: an old foe, the Philistines, who had already stolen the Ark of the Covenant (the special, sacred chest containing the Ten Commandments) from them in battle, were continuing to oppress them. So the Israelites' leader Samuel basically had to answer a very good question: Why should things be any different on the battlefield this time? The conflict would only go differently under certain conditions, he told the people. Let's take a look:

> Samuel said to all the Israelites, "If you are returning to the LORD with all your hearts, then rid yourselves of the foreign gods and the Ashtoreths and commit yourselves to the LORD and serve him only, and he will deliver you out of the hand of the Philistines." So the Israelites put away their Baals and Ashtoreths, and served the LORD only.
>
> Then Samuel said, "Assemble all Israel at Mizpah, and I will intercede with the LORD for you." When they had assembled at Mizpah, they drew water and poured it out before the LORD. On that day they fasted and there they confessed, "We have sinned against the LORD." Now Samuel was serving as leader of Israel at Mizpah.
>
> When the Philistines heard that Israel had assembled at Mizpah, the rulers of the Philistines came up to attack them. When the Israelites heard of it, they were afraid because of the Philistines. They said to Samuel, "Do not stop crying out to the LORD our God for us, that he may rescue us from the hand of the Philistines." Then Samuel took a suckling lamb and sacrificed it as a whole burnt offering to the Lord. He cried out to the LORD on Israel's behalf, and the LORD answered him.
>
> While Samuel was sacrificing the burnt offering, the Philistines drew near to engage Israel in battle. But that day the LORD thundered with loud thunder against the Philistines and threw them into such a panic that they were routed before the Israelites. The men of Israel rushed out of Mizpah and pursued the Philistines, slaughtering them along the way to a point below Beth Kar.
>
> Then Samuel took a stone and set it up between Mizpah and Shen. He named it Ebenezer, saying, "Thus far the LORD has helped us."

So the Philistines were subdued and they stopped invading Israel's territory. Throughout Samuel's lifetime, the hand of the LORD was against the Philistines. The towns from Ekron to Gath that the Philistines had captured from Israel were restored to Israel, and Israel delivered the neighboring territory from the hands of the Philistines. And there was peace between Israel and the Amorites (1 Sam. 7:3-14).

Overcoming Amnesia

It's interesting to me that before Samuel even asked God to help His people defeat their enemy, he insisted that everyone repent—turn back toward God—and confess—ask him for forgiveness for worshiping other gods. Sometimes when we're suffering great pain and grieving through a season of loss, we forget that we're still responsible for our actions, including our sinful choices and behaviors. As we've discussed, it can be very tempting to let ourselves off the hook because of our painful condition.

Whether it's abusing prescription medication, turning to alcohol, overeating or even watching TV mindlessly, we often turn to our own idols for comfort. Instead of facing our emotions head on and dealing with them before God, we self-medicate our pain. Instead of allowing others into our sorrow and receiving the comfort and assistance they offer, we retreat within ourselves. We are often our own biggest obstacle to healing and restoration. Sometimes our more honest prayer may be, "Lord, I need Your help. Please help me to get out of Your way!"

Even after they repented, the people of Israel still feared their imminent showdown with the Philistines. They begged Samuel to keep on pleading for God's help, which he did, along with sacrificing a burnt offering on their behalf. And God heard Samuel's prayers and intervened on the battlefield, throwing the pagan Philistines into such a panic that the Israelites easily defeated them. Their victory tasted all the sweeter because in that same place, exactly 20 years earlier, they had been routed and had lost the Ark.

So what did Samuel do next? He set up a stone of remembrance, a monument, basically, at the battle site. He didn't want any of the Israelites forgetting what God had done for them. Every time they saw this Ebenezer that he had erected, they would recall the way God had answered their prayers and empowered them to defeat their enemies. Perhaps the stone was similar to national historical sites in our country, places such as Gettysburg, the Alamo and Bunker Hill. You know, something like those plaques that read "George Washington slept here" or "The Union Army suffered hundreds of casualties at this site." Only, for the Israelites, the monument expressed more than just a recognition of history. Their Ebenezer also expressed their gratitude and worship for the God who loved them, forgave them and continued to deliver them. Maybe their amnesia wouldn't come back—that condition by which they seemed to forget who God was and the things He had done for them.

The kinds of things He still does for us today.

All the more reason for us to raise our own Ebenezers as a reminder of the battles God has brought us through.

Filling the Chair

After our marriage Cyd and I began the process of making a home together. We became more aware of each other's little quirks and preferences, but we were so grateful for each other that we didn't mind them. I'm sure we had our discussions about putting the toothpaste cap back on, loading the dishwasher the "right" way, and leaving the toilet seat down, but overall we felt like the most blessed people alive.

It wasn't all perfect, to be sure. One of the biggest challenges right after we married came from the way other people perceived Cyd as they continued to miss Debra and grieve her passing. We had already faced some of these moments while we were dating. Once it had become clear to people that we were together, a dear friend of mine and Debra's took it upon herself to call Debra's mother and relay the news that her son-in-law had a new girlfriend.

When this happened and we found out about it, Cyd and I were both shocked and hurt. We were still waiting on God's confirmation and blessing on our relationship at that point—we hadn't even told our own families yet. And we had already agreed that if we were going to pursue marriage, we would visit Debra's family in person and share the news. As painful as losing Debra was for all of us, the last thing Cyd and I wanted to do was have our relationship compound anyone's grief.

So even though we weren't the first to share the news with them, when Cyd and I knew that we were headed toward marriage, we went to visit Debra's parents. As strange as it may sound, there was nothing awkward about the visit. Even though Debra's parents still grieved their daughter's passing, they seemed to feel a flicker of light and life because of Cyd's presence. True to who I knew her to be, Cyd remained calm and compassionate, just being herself.

Like most people who had met her, Mrs. Smith connected with Cyd rather quickly. Shortly after we arrived and gotten introductions and small talk out of the way, Mrs. Smith headed to the kitchen to prepare refreshments. Without even asking Cyd followed her and helped her get things ready, beginning a relationship that continued until Mrs. Smith passed away on Mother's Day, sadly enough the year that Caleb, our second child, was born.

It was truly remarkable seeing Mrs. Smith gravitate to Cyd so easily, because, to tell the truth, Cyd's personality was very different from Debra's. They were each smart, beautiful and amazing in their own way, both totally in love with the Lord. But their personalities were clearly distinct from each other's.

Perhaps these differences as well as the concern that our friendship, which had been much like family, would change when I got remarried caused another friend of Debra's and mine to be a little guarded with Cyd. You might recall from my account of the accident that I had called my friend and pastor, Gordon, while I was at the crash site. He had accompanied Pastor Mike to meet us at the hospital and was present with Debra when she passed. He and his wife, Derozette, had been close friends with Debra and me; in fact, the two women had been best friends—like sisters.

Because the loss had been so devastating and Cyd obviously was not Debra, it was understandable that Derozette was guarded when it came to Cyd's presence in my life. It wasn't that she was rude to Cyd or anything; her reservation had to do with whether or not anyone could ever replace the best friend she'd lost—and no one could. So Dez remained polite but a little distant.

Shortly after Cyd and I were married, however, Dez had a very compelling dream. Close in her walk with the Lord and blessed with a prophetic gift, Dez dreamed that she had walked into a banquet room. Her closest friends were seated around a table that had one empty chair pulled up to it. Obviously, the spot that had once been Debra's was vacant. At that moment Jesus walked into the room and began walking around the table. He appeared as a man with dark hair and a beard, dressed in a multicolored robe. As He walked He shared with Dez that others would come and go from her table; however, it wasn't her responsibility to fill the empty chairs. He would fill them. When He finished speaking, He sat in Debra's empty chair.

When she awoke, Dez couldn't believe how vivid and direct her dream had been. She clearly missed Debra and knew that her best friend remained both irreplaceable and absent. And instead of working to bring someone else into her inner circle or forcing herself to get to know Cyd, Dez instead received a message from the Lord, loud and clear. She didn't have to do anything but allow Him to work in her life. He would fill that empty chair if she would simply let go and allow Him to do so.

And that's what she did. Cyd and I didn't know about her dream until several months later. Dez relaxed her stance as guardian of Debra's memory and realized that Cyd had never wanted to take anyone's place. This realization freed Dez to accept Cyd for the wonderful woman she was without comparing her to Debra or to anyone else.

Situations like these, however, reminded me of what an extraordinary woman Cyd was. She not only endured everyone else's scrutiny and evaluation, but she also remained strong and confident in who she was. She never asked me to stop talking about Debra or tried to switch the subject or draw me away from friends who had been close to Debra and me. She opened her heart to everyone who was special to me. Perhaps it's due to something Cyd told me right before we married.

She said that from her perspective, my life was a race in two stages. God had placed Debra to run alongside me for the first leg. And now he had brought Cyd into my life to run the rest of the race. God had allowed Debra to pass the baton to Cyd according to His perfect plan. "In His divine wisdom," Cyd explained, "He knew that Debra was the woman to provide what you needed for the first part of your journey. Just as He knew that I'm the woman to provide what you need for what's left."

During that first year of our marriage, Cyd and I weren't shy about sharing our story of God's amazing redemption in our lives. A friend of ours, Susan Thomas, confirmed Cyd's metaphor of running a relay with me after Debra had passed the baton to her. I'm not sure why God required me to have two wives to help me carry on His work. However, through this experience I've become fully convinced that if we trust Him, God always has a plan that is worked to perfection. His plan *always* prevails!

A Hope Awakened

In the fall of 1999, we found out that Cyd was expecting our first child. After years of wanting to be a father during my first marriage, I was so elated that God was now blessing me in this way. Cyd too was overjoyed at the prospect of motherhood and of creating a family together. She recalled her girlhood dream of being part of a family that had two loving parents. Having missed out on her relationship with her dad while growing up, Cyd felt so blessed to have found someone like me who also longed to be a parent. Like many newly married couples expecting their first child, we began to talk about names for each gender, color schemes for the baby's room and all the dreams that we had for this new life.

But it was not meant to be. Cyd miscarried the baby a few weeks later. After speaking to her doctor, our prayer was that the pregnancy would terminate naturally if the child was not going to be viable outside the womb. For three days Cyd remained in bed with her feet elevated, submitting to the miscarriage process. We were in constant prayer and worship, trusting God in the midst of this fresh loss.

It was a strange feeling—an ache for someone I never even got the chance to meet. I felt as if I had missed an appointment that would never come again. Cyd not only had to suffer emotionally but she also endured the physical pain of this tragic process.

For the next few weeks, as we grieved, the disappointment was tempered by the realization that if God had destined us to hold that child in our arms, nothing or no one could have stopped it. We resolved that we only wanted what God had for us, and we wanted it in His time. As disappointing, painful and uncertain as we felt, we knew that God's timing was always perfect.

After going back to the gynecologist, Cyd confirmed that she was healthy enough for another pregnancy. In fact, her doctor informed us that we could begin trying to have another baby within a couple of months. This event was pivotal for two reasons: It gave us greater understanding and compassion for families who'd had a similar experience, and it reinforced to Cyd how badly she wanted to become a mother.

Losing this baby stirred something deep within each of us. This made the ache of our loss that much sharper.

Remnant of Hope

Even though the doctor told us that Cyd was physically able to conceive, she and I both knew that the miracle of life only comes from our Father in heaven. For now we were forced to wait. We even had times when we wondered if He would indeed bless us with children. What if He had brought us together to love each other and to serve Him but not necessarily to raise children? Parenthood was clearly a longing in both our hearts, but we had already learned—each in our own way—that what happened was up to the Lord.

We hadn't bought many things for the baby since the miscarriage had occurred so early in the pregnancy, but the handful of items we had acquired—little onesies, tiny socks that looked as if they belonged on a doll, a white teddy bear—haunted us. As tempting as it was to put them away, out of sight, we left them where they were for the time being, tangible reminders of our loss.

Oddly enough, it helped to leave them out. For one thing, they reminded us that this hadn't been just a bad dream. Since we had never gotten to meet the baby, we sometimes wondered why we felt the loss so deeply. The baby items also provided us a remnant of hope. Not an Ebenezer—there was no victory yet—but the possibility that we would keep fighting our fears, keep praying to God and keep hoping that He would bless us with a child. Our hearts were battered, but our hope was not dead.

During this time after the miscarriage, whenever my heart ached at the loss of this precious tiny life, I reminded myself of what I had come through. On the night that Debra left this earth, I never could have imagined wanting to love another woman again, let alone meeting someone in less than a year. Debra's death had not made sense. In a matter of moments, as long as it had taken a drunk driver to run a stop sign, my life had spun 180 degrees in another direction.

When our life spins out of control, when everything changes on a dime, we still have choices. In many ways it's quite simple: We can choose life, or we can choose death. Christ came to bring us life, and, as He says, not just life but an abundant life. We can turn to Him and walk through the valley of the shadow of death toward new life. Or we can become paralyzed by the sinking weight of our emotions, the quicksand of fear, anger and sadness.

Ring of Truth

After the miscarriage I remember sitting quietly in prayer and suddenly realizing that I was fidgeting with my brand-new wedding band, turning it round and round on my finger. Maybe it was subconscious at first, but one morning I opened my eyes from my time with the Lord and saw that band. Not only was it a symbol of God's perfect, eternal love; not only was it a gift representing Cyd's love; but in that moment that gold wedding band on the ring finger of my left hand became an Ebenezer for me. If God could see me through the loss of Debra, drawing me closer to Him than ever before, and then bring Cyd into my life, He would not desert us now.

I shared with you how I identified with Isaac in the situation in which God had told his father, Abraham, to sacrifice him. Well, now I knew something of what Abraham must have felt when God told him that he would not only be a father but the father of a nation. Something had been awakened inside my heart—the desire to be a daddy. Not to a nation of people but simply to one little boy or girl. Abraham knew that ache. As the years passed by and his body aged, as he watched his wife, Sarah, age as well, leaving her childbearing years behind, Abraham must have wrestled with doubt.

It wasn't possible at their age—and yet God continued to tell him that he would father a son. And then, of course, Sarah conceived in her old age. It sounds biologically and scientifically impossible. But with God all things are possible.

If God could give Abraham and Sarah a baby, then I knew that He could do the same for me and Cyd. So I kept praying, twisting my wedding ring. It wasn't a rock of remembrance or a plaque on the wall, but it became my Ebenezer, a reminder of what God can do: the seemingly impossible.

No matter what you're going through, during the process of restoration, you will face setbacks. They may be great or small, but either way, their impact sends you reeling. During these times, look back on what God has done for you. Remember how far you've come. Go for a walk, and find a rock that will fit in the palm of your hand. Make this rock your Ebenezer, something you can hold in your palm while you pray and ask God for help, trusting in His love and goodness.

Finally, remember the words of the old hymn "Come Thou Fount of Every Blessing." Let the second verse become your prayer:

Here I raise my Ebenezer;
Here by Thy great help I've come;
And I hope, by Thy good pleasure,
Safely to arrive at home.

No matter how disappointing your setback or devastating an additional loss may be, just remember that God will see you through it. You can move through new losses and painful disappointments by remembering how God has delivered you in the past. Because He's been faithful and has never abandoned you, you can trust Him in the midst of present unexpected trials. Best of all, you can trust Him with your future.

RESTORE AND RENEW

1. As you reflect back over your life, how has God consistently provided for you and protected you from harm? When do you question His presence in the midst of painful circumstances?

2. Fill in the blanks in these questions: "I wonder where God was when _____ happened? Why would He have allowed _____ to happen to me?"

3. What's been difficult for you to start again in the aftermath of loss and heartache? Are there relationships, activities and places that you still refuse to engage? Why?

4. What Ebenezers, or souvenirs of God's goodness, have you established in your life up until now?

5. Choose a new Ebenezer to commemorate the new thing that God is doing in you during this season of restoration. It could be a stone you pick up on a walk, a card someone sent you or a work of art you've made or purchased. Whatever it is, choose something that you will see regularly, if not daily, and that will remind you of God's ongoing goodness in your life.

RECONNECT AND REVIVE

Lord, thank You for lifting me up and restoring me to new life. I raise my own Ebenezer as a remembrance of this season in which You transformed my pain into Your power. I trust You, Father, and I will continue to follow You. Amen.

9

Celebrate Your Anniversary: Delighting in Days of Redemption

Cyd and I love holidays, especially Christmas and Easter with their extra special significance in celebrating the birth and resurrection of our Savior. The decorations and traditions, the beautiful music—and let's not forget the food! You can't grow up in Louisiana and live in Texas without enjoying some of the most delicious home cooking this side of heaven! Whether it's red beans and rice with sausage, potato salad, prime Angus beef or a big pot of chicken-and-sausage gumbo, you can't beat the smells, tastes and full bellies around our extended family's table.

In addition to those big holidays, we really enjoy celebrating our personal days of remembrance too. Cyd's birthday is always special and requires intensive celebration for at least 24 hours if not for an entire week. And on our anniversary I love taking her to the restaurant where I proposed—and she always makes me order chocolate-covered strawberries, of course! Our sons' birthdays are also incredibly special, perhaps more so because of the history leading up to their arrivals.

When people have experienced incredible loss and overcome a variety of obstacles, as we have, the days of commemorating God's goodness become even more meaningful. We realize that even though painful emotions may have saturated our mind and body, we still have a choice about their lasting effect on our soul. We come to understand that even though it seems totally, absolutely impossible to imagine seeing anything good come from our loss, God makes it possible.

But ours is a God who wastes nothing; in fact, there's a Hebrew name for God, *Ha'al Shemaays eyes qumin*, meaning exactly that: God wastes nothing. He can transform anything—and I mean anything—into something beautiful, life affirming and glorious for His kingdom. It may even be what He does best. When Adam and Eve rebelled in the garden, God revealed His passionate pursuit of relationship with His earthly children in other ways than He had done at first.

When His people, the children of Israel, wandered away from Him time after time, God compared His broken heart to that of a good man who marries a prostitute—even as she continues to betray him with her customers. For extra emphasis, God revealed this metaphor through the life of His prophet Hosea and Hosea's unfaithful wife, Gomer. But God never gave up on His people.

Eventually, of course, God sent His Son to the earth as a baby boy, who grew up and then revealed His true identity as the Messiah, the promised Savior of God's people. Christ ended up as an innocent man who was killed by being hung on a cross with common thieves and criminals. But, as you know, the story wasn't over. Three days after Jesus was killed—the tomb was empty!

God works this amazing thread of resurrection power into the design of every life. He transforms our scars of battle into sacred emblems of beauty. If we're willing to trust Him, we can experience restoration in ways that once seemed impossible to us. The fabric of our life's garment may seem torn and frayed, ripped and soiled, but God repairs the tears, patches the holes and washes us until we're clean and pure.

We only have to let Him.

Double Trouble

A few months after our miscarriage, God demonstrated His faithfulness once again, as we became pregnant for the second time. We were overjoyed and thankful. To our surprise, the doctor informed us that there were two sacks in Cyd's womb and estimated our due date to be January 2, 2001. Twins, oh my goodness! Cyd and I were literally speechless to think about having two babies at once.

However, our doctor warned us that one of the sacs looked a lot weaker than the other one and that most likely we would experience what was called "the vanishing twin syndrome" in which the weaker membrane becomes absorbed by the stronger one. We indicated that we understood but continued to pray for both babies, regardless of the way the situation appeared. Unfortunately, in time it was revealed that we had indeed lost one baby. We prayed that this would allow the remaining baby the strength it needed to grow and develop to full term.

The first trimester was brutal on Cyd's little body, as morning sickness ravaged her on a daily basis. She had intense Braxton Hicks contractions—irregular false contractions that can cause great discomfort. When Cyd noticed them, so did I. While we knew that some women barely noticed them, we remained concerned and vigilant over everything, as first-time parents are prone to do.

One day Cyd began spotting. Since our prior pregnancy that had resulted in a miscarriage had followed this pattern, we were naturally concerned. When we went to the doctor, we were told that everything was okay but that Cyd needed to stay in bed for the next few days and keep her feet elevated. The spotting continued, and we knew we had a fight on our hands.

On the third day of bed rest with no apparent victory in sight, I sat on the side of the bed in which Cyd was lying. I began to call to the Lord on behalf of our child, and in desperation I cried out, "Lord, please speak to us—I know that Your Word has something to say about this situation." While making that declaration, I randomly opened my Bible. As I looked down, the Scripture passage that stood out to me was Psalm 147:

> Praise the LORD! For it is good to sing praises to our God; for it is pleasant, and praise is beautiful.
>
> The LORD builds up Jerusalem; He gathers together the outcasts of Israel. He heals the brokenhearted and binds up their wounds. He counts the number of the stars; He calls them all by name. Great is our Lord, and mighty

in power; His understanding is infinite. The LORD lifts up the humble; He casts the wicked down to the ground.

Sing to the LORD with thanksgiving; sing praises on the harp to our God, who covers the heavens with clouds, who prepares rain for the earth, who makes grass to grow on the mountains. He gives to the beast its food, and to the young ravens that cry.

He does not delight in the strength of the horse; He takes no pleasure in the legs of a man. The LORD takes pleasure in those who fear Him, in those who hope in His mercy.

Praise the LORD, O Jerusalem! Praise your God, O Zion! For He has strengthened the bars of your gates; He has blessed your children within you (Ps. 147:1-13, *NKJV*).

After I read the thirteenth verse, I stopped reading and started praising. I turned to Cyd and said, "The Lord has spoken; listen to this: 'He has strengthened the bars of your gates; He has blessed your children within you.' Cyd, this is our word! Right now we need the gate at your cervix to keep this child from being released before its time. You have children within you."

We felt so hopeful, and the joy of the Lord filled the room as we began to declare that the "bars of Cyd's gates were strengthened" and that they would not open before their time. God had given us a word that we would use to stand on during this season.

We also found great solace in another verse: "I will rebuke the devourer for your sakes, and he shall not destroy the fruits of your ground; neither shall your vine cast her fruit before the time in the field, saith the LORD of hosts" (Mal. 3:11, *KJV*). God's Word was alive and powerful, and the more we declared it, the more our faith increased. This verse was our rallying cry each time Cyd felt ill or experienced something that didn't seem ordinary. After that word was released to us, the Lord began to bring other couples into our lives who needed the same word for the same type of situation.

The Lord did strengthen the bars of Cyd's gates, and neither did her vine cast her fruit before its time, because we made it through the first and second trimesters. The day we heard the baby's heartbeat was so exciting. As her belly grew, that small bump seemed to swallow up Cyd's little body. We later found out that we were having a son, much to my delight.

From the moment we heard his little heartbeat, I began reading to our son, whose name the Lord eventually told us: "Seth," which means "appointed." This name is the one that Adam and Eve chose for their third son after they rebelled against God and had to leave Eden. Their first two children, Cain and Abel—well, you probably know how that turned out. After experiencing the devastating heartbreak of losing their home in paradise due to their own sinful disobedience, Adam and Eve faced another great loss. Not only did they lose their second-born son, but since he died at the hands of his brother, they lost their older son as well. Naturally, they were distraught with grief.

But their story was not over. With Abel murdered by Cain, who was subsequently marked by God and sent into exile, there was no one to continue the legacy of Adam and Eve—not to mention the human race. Then God allowed Eve to conceive by her husband to deliver a son, whom they named Seth. God indeed "appointed" their son's arrival, just as He was now doing for us.

Never Give Up

When we experience setbacks during our restoration, it can be disheartening to feel as if we're losing hope once again. We regain our footing, step out in faith, make some progress—but then something causes us to stumble. Our fragile hope, the trust in God we had been working so diligently to restore, seems to shatter along the same old cracks. But before we despair, we need to remember that this is not unusual. In fact, it's unusual if it *doesn't* happen.

We live in a world that's been stained by human sinfulness. But we also live by faith, since we are loved by a God for whom nothing is impossible. Our Father has not abandoned us, but neither has He promised us a problem-free life. In fact, James tells us, "Consider it pure joy, my brothers and sisters, whenever you face trials of many kinds, because you know that the testing of your faith produces perseverance. Let perseverance finish its work so that you may be mature and complete, not lacking anything" (1:2-4).

So when we're in rebuilding mode spiritually, we must be careful not to expect that we won't suffer again. We must simply allow our past trials and losses to make us stronger, more mature in our faith and closer to God. As when Eve lamented the loss of her children, we must remember that Seth, God's appointed one, is right around the corner.

The gift of our Seth certainly strengthened Cyd's and my souls. God had appointed this child for us after the loss of our first and the most recent incident. As Cyd's pregnancy progressed, I would lie next to her in bed or kneel down beside her as she sat on the sofa, getting as close to her tummy as I could, and I would read, talk or sing to our precious little boy.

One of my favorite songs to sing to Seth in the womb was this one:

> Little Seth Ryan loves living, living,
>   Little Seth Ryan loves living bread.
> Little Seth Ryan loves living, living,
>   Little Seth Ryan loves living bread.
> You've got to raise up your hands, fall on your face;
>   The Holy Ghost is going to shake this place.
> Raise up your hands, fall on your face,
>   The Holy Ghost is going to shake this place.

My conversations and songs with Seth could amount to a couple of hours over the course of a day.

As Cyd's belly grew, Seth seemed to be very alert in her womb. In the later part of the pregnancy, he and I would play footsies. We could literally see the small impression of Seth's little foot pressing against the side of Cyd's belly. I would take my index finger and gently move it from the top to the bottom of his tiny little foot. He would quickly pull it away. Then about 15 or 20 seconds later, we would see the little impression slowly return to another position. We would play that game back and forth until Seth would become bored and keep his foot to himself. It was a special time of bonding for the three of us.

Cyd was more beautiful during this season than I had ever seen her. People often commented on how a woman of her small stature could have such a big belly. It looked as if the slightest touch to her tummy would cause it to burst. But her size only made her more radiant. We received many opportunities for laughter with our family and friends during this time.

By the end of the second trimester, Cyd launched into full-blown nesting activities. She displayed enormous energy in the flurry of activity because of her drive to get everything in order well before Seth's January due date.

Watching and listening to Cyd during her preparation mode, I struggled to keep up with her. Her exuberance zapped the energy right out of me, even if the only thing I was doing was watching sports on TV! I would say to her, "Girl, sit down! You're making me tired just watching you!" and we'd both burst into laughter.

There was no question that I had pregnancy sympathy for her. We both ate Honey Nut Crunch cereal as if it were the last food source on the earth. She craved catfish from Cracker Barrel, and we practically lived at a cafeteria-styled restaurant called Luby's. The only problem was that while Cyd's calories were revealing themselves in a big belly because of a baby, my calories were simply revealing themselves in a big belly—period.

Both of us were definitely celebrating becoming parents, in part because we knew what it meant to lose that privilege. Occasionally we would see spotting, but we continued to declare the verses we'd been given, Psalm 147:13 and Malachi 3:11, and God's grace continued to abound.

The Time Is Now

When we've lost something or someone dear to us, it often makes us more grateful for the blessings we do have. Nothing can make up for our losses. As I've mentioned earlier, I'm convinced God shares our heartache when we grieve. But our past losses should not blind us to what we have in the present—and what awaits us in the future.

After our miscarriage, our baby Seth became all the more precious to us. We remained apprehensive, and we experienced moments of fear, but that's when we would cling to God and the words of truth He had given to us.

As the Thanksgiving holiday neared, I packed my bag for the hospital stay. Cyd's nesting instincts included making a to-do list in early October in preparation for the baby. Having my bag packed allowed her to check one item off the list and helped keep that list from driving me crazy. Besides, I didn't want to be unprepared—in the back of my mind, I wondered if God had finished writing the testimony of our lives, or was He still up to something?

Christmas was just around the corner. On the morning of December 16 I informed Cyd that I was going to drive to the country to check on a piece of property that we had under development. The drive was two hours round trip into southeast Collin County. As I prepared to leave the house, Cyd lay on the sofa. It had seemed over the last several days that Seth had not been as active in the womb as at previous times. But our concerns faded once again as we reminded ourselves of God's promises from His Word. So, preparing to leave for the day, I kissed Cyd on the forehead and said, "Be sure you call me if you need anything."

I had been driving for about 25 or 30 minutes when my phone rang; it was Cyd. She said, "Honey, I'm really having some bad Braxton Hicks contractions." Now I'm no expert, but I figured that with my wife in her thirty-eighth week of her pregnancy, most likely these were not Braxton Hicks contractions. No, these were more like the real deal contractions!

"Girl, you're in labor—there's no way you should be having Braxton Hicks this late," I said. "Have you timed them yet?"

"No," she replied, "but I sure am hungry—and way too tired to prepare a meal." Once my wife had food on her mind, it would have to be addressed soon.

"I'll fix us something once I'm back, baby," I said. "But time those contractions and call me back, okay?"

A few minutes later Cyd called and with a still, calm voice, seemingly unaware of any concern, said, "Honey, it looks like the contractions are three minutes apart."

"Three minutes apart!" I shouted. "Check again, that can't be right—'cause if it is, you are about to have a baby!" I held on the line until Cyd timed the contractions again.

"Uh, yes, they are three minutes apart," she exclaimed.

By this time I was looking for the next exit off the freeway to make a U-turn.

"Honey, I'm on my way. Stay as calm as you can," I said, aware that I was the one who was about to lose it. I was 30 minutes from home, and my wife was having contractions three minutes apart!

I was about to hang up, but Cyd was still not convinced, apparently. "Honey," she said, "can you drive through Wendy's and get me a burger?"

"Well, okay," I said, confident that I was going to be eating that burger while she was in labor.

Fifteen minutes into my return trip, Cyd called again, this time informing me that the contractions were down to two minutes apart. As crazy or unbiblical as this may sound, I immediately began praying that the Lord would blind the eyes of any police officers and cause radar detectors to malfunction. My little Toyota 4Runner was flying down the interstate.

Several scenarios flashed before my eyes: When I walked into the house, Cyd would be lying on the sofa with the umbilical cord still attached holding a little baby boy yelling his lungs out. Or I would make it home in time, but during the car ride to the hospital, the baby would be born. Fear gripped me as I prayed, "Lord, please don't let Cyd have this child until we are at the hospital."

The 25- to 30-minute drive seemed like an eternity. When I finally walked through the door, Cyd said in a very matter-of-fact tone, "The contractions are now one and a half minutes apart—hey, did you stop by Wendy's?"

"No, girl," I said. "We'll get you something on the way to the hospital." Again, I knew there would be no single with cheese and extra pickle for my sweetheart. I found as many ways as I could to distract her from thinking about that thick, juicy hamburger.

I quickly grabbed the suitcases and loaded up the car. As I helped Cyd into the vehicle, she began to assure me that we were wasting our time bringing those suitcases to the hospital. She shared a story of a friend who had gone in twice, thinking she was in labor, only to find out that her contractions were false alarms. This stuck in Cyd's head to the point that she seemed totally oblivious to the urgency of our situation.

I took a completely different route than we normally did going to the hospital for the sole purpose of avoiding the hamburger joint. She was not fooled; Cyd made her objections known, but this was the least of my concerns. The eight-minute jaunt to the hospital happened in a flash. We were getting ready to have a baby.

The time had finally come.

Date with Destiny

God and His timing had gotten us this far, and I wasn't about to doubt His faithfulness now. There we were at the hospital, and I was feeling very confident about the situation. As we piled into the elevator, Cyd expressed her embarrassment at how I was overreacting with the entire luggage thing and how she couldn't believe that I hadn't gotten her anything to eat.

When we arrived on the floor for labor and delivery, a nurse directed us to a room where Cyd would be checked. As we hauled our luggage into the room, Cyd was given further instructions to go into the bathroom and put on a hospital gown. I went in with her to give her some assistance.

As she transitioned into the hospital gown, I heard her say, "Oh, mannn!"

"What, honey?" I exclaimed.

She responded, "I'm all wet."

The moment of truth had arrived—her water had broken! There was no way they would send her home now. But for some reason, she still didn't seem to get it. Or maybe she was just in denial now that the time was at hand. As much as she wanted this baby, Cyd couldn't exactly be looking forward to going into labor.

"Sweetie, have you seen the car keys?" I asked her.

"They're on the couch," Cyd replied. "What do you need those for?"

"I'm going down to the car." I responded. "To get the baby bag."

"Why would you do that?" she asked. "And when are you going to get me something to eat?"

I couldn't help but laugh. "Honey," I said, "your water has broken, you are about to have a baby, and there will be no burger for you until after he's here."

Cyd didn't believe me until the nurse walked in and politely confirmed to her that she was not going home because she indeed was about to have a baby.

The nurse proceeded to check Cyd and informed us that she had already dilated to three centimeters. An hour later, around nine in the evening, Cyd was at six centimeters, and by ten o'clock, at nine centimeters. At that time the hospital staff called the doctor, and the nurse hinted that our child would come within the hour.

After everyone left the room, I clasped Cyd's hand in mine, and I told her how proud I was of her and how excited I was that Seth was on the way. But I didn't know how to break a certain piece of news that had come to me as a startling realization, because I knew she was in so much pain. So I took a deep breath, swallowed and calmly told her, "Cyd, I'm not sure how to tell you this, but, Seth won't be born until tomorrow."

"Huh, what are you talking about?" she asked in a very defensive tone.

I continued, "Seth won't be born until tomorrow—December 17."

Puzzled for a moment, then catching her breath, the light bulb went on as her eyes acknowledged the impact of my revelation. We both were in awe, knowing that we were about to see another facet of God's beautiful redemptive plan. You see, Cyd understood that, for the last three years, on December 17, the date of the accident, and on the eighteenth, the day Debra was declared deceased, God had always done something to remind me that He really was in charge.

Seth was not due until January 2, but here we were in labor on December 16, nearing the anniversary of the most devastating day of my life. Now it was about to become one of the most joyful.

Nonetheless, nothing could prepare us for what would happen the next three and a half hours. Cyd's doctor was out on her own maternity leave, so another doctor, a partner in the same practice, was designated to perform our delivery. Finally, around one o'clock in the morning, Cyd dilated the last centimeter. By that time the doctor was still not present, and the nurses kept calling him and getting no response.

For the next two hours we could see the crown of Seth's head in the birth canal. Cyd was in excruciating pain and completely exhausted. The epidural she'd had shortly after we'd arrived had started to wear off and was no longer providing the relief she needed. I was praying to the Lord with all my heart.

When the doctor finally arrived, we were in a state of emergency; Seth's blood pressure was beginning to drop rapidly. Without knowing or asking anyone whether Cyd's epidural was still in effect or whether she had been localized with an anesthetic, in his haste to avert a tragedy, he performed an episiotomy on Cyd. She screamed a horrific scream as the doctor cut into her flesh, reached into her cervix, and with forceps pulled Seth's head through the birth canal.

To me it seemed as if everything in the world stopped for that moment. Amidst the pain, the anguish, the fear, the anticipation—there he was. As his little body entered the world, Seth started crying at the top of his lungs. And overcome with relief and joy, I began to worship the Lord God Almighty as great big tears of joy swelled up in my eyes and rolled down the sides of my cheeks.

Cyd was still in shock and in too much pain to truly enjoy the moment. It was 3:34 A.M., Sunday, December 17, 2000. The great and merciful God had redeemed the very day. The day that had initiated what had once caused me the greatest pain had now become the day of my greatest joy. I was a father for the very first time! Seth, the one whom God had appointed for us on this appointed day, had arrived!

The Weight of Glory

As they placed Seth on the weighing scale, he was still screaming with all the strength he could muster. I eased up next to the scale, stooped over until my mouth was near his tiny little ear and began to sing our song: "Little Seth Ryan loves living, living, little Seth Ryan loves living bread . . ." As I continued to sing just above a whisper, Seth stopped crying, turned his head slightly to the left and gazed toward me. My little buddy recognized his daddy's voice and the song I had been singing to him for months while he was still in the womb. At that moment I could have shouted from the highest mountain, because I felt as if I was on top of the world.

The first person I called was our friend Jay Hellwig, who had been sitting in the labor and delivery waiting room along with his wife, Jill, for most of the evening in anticipation of Seth's arrival.

"Jay, our little boy is here, and he's healthy and beautiful!" I exclaimed through sobs and tears of joy. We rejoiced together. Next I called Reggie and Tia Texada, my brother and his wife, who had arrived at the hospital during the delivery process. Reggie had been a source of strength to me during my season of singleness. He will always have a special place in my heart.

After calling a few other special friends, I called my parents, Cyd's mom and then Debra's parents. When Debra's mom, Eunice, answered the phone, I said, "Mrs. Smith, I'm calling to let you know that I'm a daddy now! Cyd just gave birth to Seth Ryan Texada!" In her typical sweet fashion, she replied, "Ohhhhh, baaaby, we are so happy for you! God is good. Tell your beautiful wife that we are so proud of her."

Then I placed a call to Pastors Mike and Kathy. "Pastor, we've got us a boy, and guess what today is? It's the four-year anniversary of the accident that resulted in Debra's death."

Pastor Mike replied through tears, "Ricky, we are so proud of you and Cyd, and we rejoice in God's goodness to you." Later that morning Pastor announced to the church that we had welcomed our baby boy into the world, and he shared the significance of the day for us. The congregation erupted in shouts of praise.

If anyone could appreciate the extreme low that God had redeemed into a jubilant high, Pastor Mike surely could. He and his wife along with my entire church family had walked with me through my grief, and now they would celebrate with me in my joy. The phone calls placed and received seemed to be never ending; people all over the nation celebrated God's day of redemption with me.

Once Cyd was tended to and ready, they brought our son to her. As she held him close, I kissed her on the forehead, so grateful for this beautiful gift that had come from my heavenly Father through her.

That moment still makes my head spin even now. Four years earlier, my world was turned upside down. The plans I had made for my future appeared to be destroyed, but God's plans were moving according to His schedule. My plan had appeared to be tracking with His until that dreadful night of December 17, 1996. I came to understand that the events that had unfolded in my life had happened in the right sequence, at the right time, in the right place. It was as if pieces of a puzzle had come together. Although I couldn't see it, God's purpose for me had been fashioned before the world began.

Await Something Great

When I look at my life now, I marvel at how normal it seems on the surface. Often people meeting Cyd and me for the first time compliment me on what a beautiful family I have, and I couldn't agree more. However, it's all the more beautiful because I know the price that was paid for what Cyd and I enjoy now. I know the sometimes-bumpy road and all its twists and turns, many of which I'm sharing with you here. The bountiful blessings that God has bestowed on our marriage, our sons and our ministry still amaze me.

While many blessings have been poured out over the years on me and Cyd and our family, I'll never forget the feeling of having a day of painful remembrance transformed into the literal birth date of new life. God vividly redeemed the painful anniversary date with the joy of a new baby boy. Although we can never forget our losses, we often see them redeemed and transformed into blessings.

So much can change when we wait on God's timing.

Whether the anniversary date of your greatest loss or simply a painful reminder of what you've lost, your Father can turn our painful memories inside out. He delights in giving us good gifts and redeems our losses in ways we can't imagine or anticipate. During restoration we must never forget the people and possibilities we've lost, but similarly, we must never forget what God can do when we rely on Him. Yes, we remember the anniversary of past losses, but we must also allow God to transform those wounds by creating new memories of joy and celebration.

And when we are in the in-between time, we wait on Him. We grieve; we grow; we get stronger; we grow closer to God. And we remain patient to see what amazing beauty God will produce out of our pain. This is simply what God does because of who He is—He transforms misery into mystery, trials into triumph, and loss into legacy.

So if you're hurting, if you're wondering how God could ever transform your greatest loss into lasting treasure, just wait. Keep on keeping on, and wait on the Lord. Expect that He will do something miraculous, impossible or beautiful beyond what you can imagine. Just wait and see. As the psalmist says so beautifully,

> I remain confident of this: I will see the goodness of the LORD in the land of the living. Wait for the LORD; be strong and take heart and wait for the LORD (27:13-14).

RESTORE AND RENEW

1. Make a list of the current blessings in your life. Spend some time in prayer, thanking God for each one. Which ones have emerged as a result of what you've lost?
2. How has God rewarded your willingness to trust Him to produce healing and restoration in your life?
3. What are you currently waiting for and asking God to provide?
4. When you reflect back on times when you've suffered, how has your perspective changed? What has God revealed to you since those initial losses?
5. Who are you currently confiding in and asking to support you with prayer and encouragement?

RECONNECT AND REVIVE

Dear God, I want to continue moving forward in this new season of growth and healing. Thank You for the many ways, large and small, in which I see Your hand at work. Please allow me to look back only so that I can see how far You have brought me. Amen.

Share Your Story: Allowing God to Transform Your Theme

I'll never forget the first time Cyd and I took our boys to an art museum. The boys were amazed to discover that people, also known as artists, painted pictures that were framed and hung on walls so that other people, like us, could come through and stare at them. Of course Caleb explained it this way: "Sorta like how you put the pictures we draw on the fridge so that everybody can see them!"

On a visit to Washington, DC, one painting in particular captured our interest: an enormous mural located in our nation's Capitol Building that depicted the signing of the Declaration of Independence. The most prominent figure is George Washington, who stands next to Richard Spaight of North Carolina as he signs the declaration. Benjamin Franklin, the oldest signer of the document, is seated in the center of the portrait. Other recognizable faces are James Madison and Alexander Hamilton. They all came to life in one big ongoing scene unrolled before us. The funny thing is that the boys didn't realize it was a mural at first. They were fascinated by the corner of the painting that was in front of their four-to five-foot eye level. Then Seth started backing up and taking in more of the enormous scene.

He backed up a few more feet and then a few more. Cyd and I watched out of the corners of our eyes, smiling to each other and waiting. Sure enough, Seth was soon backed up all the way across the room, about 40 or 50 feet away. His eyes got big, and we heard him say, *"Wow!"*

Just then Caleb looked up and realized that his brother was missing. He looked around, spotted him and ran to stand beside him. Both boys stood marveling at the epic work of art depicting history and the men who had shaped our nation and ultimately our lives.

"Hey, Dad!" Caleb yelled. "Come see how big this thing is!"

Cyd and I laughed and headed over to take in the view from our sons' perspective. The mural looked entirely different from there, all the small details intricately blending into each other to form one giant panoramic scene. I'd seen this mural before, but something about seeing it through the boys' eyes made it new again for me.

The way we see our own stories works like this.

Usually we can't see how our painful chapters fit into the story of our lives until we have some distance from them. Then we can see a bigger picture, one with connections to other people and events that we hadn't noticed before. One with unexpected colors and surprising intersections.

One with God's brushstrokes all over it.

Tell It Like It Is

From the beginning of our relationship, Cyd and I had never tried to hide the way God had brought us together. Seeing His involvement in the way we became reacquainted and the unique timing of it was just too conspicuous not to notice. She and I were already committed to living for the Lord and following Him and His ways as obediently as possible. But to have seen the unimaginable way He brought us together—it still leaves us humbled and astonished.

And please understand: God's faithfulness and goodness to me and to Cyd were not the result of an isolated event. Our blessing is unique and it's ours, of course, but God was not rewarding us because we had earned His favor. *He was blessing us because of who He is.* The same way He will continue to bless you as His beloved child. And like any grateful child, we become compelled to glorify God by sharing what He's done for us with other people.

In fact, if we look closely in the Scriptures at the individuals Jesus encountered, especially those who were forever changed— healed, forgiven, restored—by meeting Him, we will notice that they felt compelled to tell others about their experiences. The blind man. The woman at the well. The lepers. Jesus wanted them to feel the freedom that comes from being healed and restored, but He also wanted them to remember the source of their restoration. Though the Scriptures don't directly indicate that all of those touched by Jesus shared their story, we can conclude that they often did. Several times Scripture records the news of His great deeds spread far and wide (see Matt. 9:23-31). When others became aware of the great things Jesus was doing, it gave them hope that they too could experience the love and healing power of God.

Being a pastor, it was natural for me to share my testimony and the story of Cyd's and my relationship with others. Similarly, she felt the same level of comfort with describing to others the unique circumstances that had brought us together as well as her feelings about those events. Because of the dramatic nature of our story, we were often asked by various friends and ministry partners to share what God had done for us. In virtually every occasion when we did, people told us how blessed they were by hearing our story.

Many individuals who had lost loved ones received a spark of hope by hearing how God had blessed us. Others simply celebrated and worshiped Him for His goodness with us. Some found the strength to keep going and to wait on God to reveal His plan for them.

Despite our willingness to share our story whenever God revealed an opportunity, Cyd and I did encounter a couple of potential pitfalls. One concern we had, as I mentioned earlier, is that she and I would receive the attention, glory and honor that can belong only to the Lord. We tried to be very clear with people that the only thing we did to enjoy God's blessings was to keep stepping out in faith, relying on Him day to day and hour by hour. We experienced God's faithfulness because we faced our pain and put loving Him before our own comfort, happiness or convenience.

The other potential snare had to do with Debra. On one hand, it's always a glorious way to remember her and her love for God by sharing about my love for her—as well as my devastation when she died. However, I also realized early on that I didn't want Cyd to feel as if she were always competing with Debra. It's only human to be curious and maybe even a little jealous of your spouse's former flames. But when that person is your husband's deceased wife, things get more than a little tricky.

Chick flicks and romance novels often encourage us to put loved ones we've lost on a pedestal—to view them as an untouchable ideal that we sugarcoat in our memories. Classic films like *Vertigo* as well as more recent ones like *Ghost* and *P.S. I Love You* portray the way such a loss becomes compounded when the deceased spouse suddenly becomes a saint in the survivor's mind. Widowers and widows abound in love stories in which they can't make peace with the loss of their beloved partner. Depending on whether it's an independent, art-house tragedy film, or one on Lifetime with a feel-good ending, these stories create love triangles that transcend death.

Maybe I'm exaggerating, but I think you know what I'm talking about. This tendency to venerate a lost loved one can undermine the healthiest of relationships when a spouse continues to compare his or her new love with the one he or she once knew. The deceased becomes a virtual saint, the surviving spouse setting impossible standards to live up to since they're always romanticized by memory and emotion.

With this possibility in mind, I worked hard to remain vigilant and aware of my feelings and words. I love Cyd for who she is, not for how she is or isn't like Debra. Fortunately, Cyd has always respected and loved Debra for loving me during the first leg of my race. With her confidence firmly secured in Christ, Cyd knows that He is the source of her identity. As I've shared in prior chapters, Cyd has handled the comparisons, judgments and scrutiny of others with poise, dignity and humility.

Cyd sees this story not as *my* story only but as *our* story. It also helps that she is not naturally a jealous person. Sure, she doesn't want me eyeballing other women and doesn't like anyone flirting my way, but overall she is anchored in her relationship with God and confident in my love for her. I have appreciated this aspect of her even more as we have shared the story of how our Father brought us together. Without this kind of strength of character, trust and security within Cyd, I could never write this book or even share our story fully.

Each time Cyd and I share the story of what God has done in our lives, we affirm our love for one another, and more importantly, we glorify our Father. Yes, it also honors Debra's memory and continues her legacy of faith, but even these effects of our sharing ultimately lead back to God. He is the master story-maker, the author and finisher of our faith, the Alpha and the Omega, the Creator who knew us before we were ever born and who knows how our story will end.

Holding Out for a Hero

When we share our stories of healing and restoration with others, we affirm the significance of what we've lost, offer hope to those in need and celebrate our reliance on God for the power to move forward. While God's Word and the presence of His Spirit comfort and sustain us, our Father also knows that we need other forms of tangible encouragement. There's something undeniably powerful about having another man or woman look us in the eye and open their hearts to us. Pain connects us to each other as surely as our ability to love, which is ultimately the only balm that can heal us.

In other words, we need each other's stories—for connection, hope and examples of God performing the impossible. It's why we love to hear a good story when we're children. We need stories of hope to feed our faith.

In fact, one of the joys of being a parent is seeing familiar stories anew through the eyes of my children. When our boys were younger, I loved reading them bedtime stories, especially some of my favorite Bible stories, like those of Noah, Moses, David, Joseph, Joshua, Gideon, Ruth and Naomi, Esther and Daniel. These people are not only great saints of the Christian faith, but also they are heroes with action-packed, epic-adventure lives that rival any video game or superhero movie.

These men and women faced life-threatening danger, faith-testing trials and God-revealing miracles that continue to inspire us. The odds seemed stacked against them, yet they persevered and triumphed by trusting God and remaining obedient to Him. They were underdogs and outcasts, runts and rebels, dreamers and deceivers. Others bet against them, falsely accused them, sold them into slavery, threatened to kill them or abandoned them in jail—*but these heroes of the faith never gave up.*

My sons love these stories for the same reasons that you and I love them. We may not know how we will ever recover from the loss of our loved one, but then we remember Ruth. We can't imagine being able to pay all our bills and get out of debt, but then Joseph comes to mind. Office politics and unethical supervisors discourage us until we recall the courage of David squaring off against an arrogant giant named Goliath. What we face feels overwhelming and all-consuming to us in the present. But God is bigger and more powerful than anything we're up against.

Others' stories remind us of this important truth more vividly than any scientific proof, theological explanation or philosophical ideal. While data, facts and concepts are important, we long for connection with other human beings. We long to know what they've been through, how they got through it and how it changed them. We're strengthened, refreshed and motivated once again to keep going. If others can do it, then so can we.

Part of the way God sustains and encourages us is by bringing other believers into our lives at just the right time. When we hear the testimony of someone who has faced a loss or a crisis similar to our own, we experience new hope. We feel less alone knowing that we're not the only person to endure such heartache. We feel relieved to know that our emotional response is similar to what someone else has felt. And we gain courage knowing that others have been able to move through the wreckage and to rebuild their lives. We're reminded that God is faithful, loving and good—that He has not abandoned us and never will.

As we grow and move through our pain, we share our stories so that we can give life to others. We tell our stories so that God can be honored and glorified, so that other people can hear of His goodness, mercy and love. We share our stories so that we can regain perspective on who we are, on who God is and on the amazing epic story that He's authoring based on the individual chapters of each of our lives.

A Good Ending

When our injury paralyzes us, it's like being stuck in a traffic jam on the highway. All of a sudden every car in every lane comes to a complete stop. Minutes pass and then more, and soon a half hour has gone by. We don't understand what the holdup could be. We were driving along at the speed limit, anticipating the arrival at our destination, when suddenly everything came to a grinding halt. The road curves ahead and then disappears on the other side of a long hill. It feels as if traffic will never resume, that we will never get going again and reach our original destination.

Finally, the vehicles around us begin to crawl along, and eventually we're diverted to an exit with an alternate route, a detour. At the top of the exit ramp, we can see the other side of the hill, and we realize that a hulking semi has jackknifed and blocked all the lanes. We couldn't see this obstacle before; we only knew that we had been forced to stop. But now we've gained a different perspective and can see above and beyond the problem. Before long, we're on our way and traveling at normal speed again.

When we get into these kinds of situations, we usually try to warn friends and family who we know might travel this same route. We give them a heads-up and encourage them to take another way. Or we give them an estimate, based on our own experience, as to how long it will take them to move through the area.

Whether in life or on the highway, we help each other on our journeys based on what we've experienced.

Forgive me if this metaphor seems obvious, but so often when our life loss or personal crisis brings us to a stop, we can't see beyond it. We can't imagine how we'll ever start going again. We don't understand how this could be happening or how we'll ever reach our destination. So we have to wait and surrender control. We have to trust God with removing the obstacle and empowering us to continue. We have to rely on Him to guide us to a new route, one we probably did not anticipate taking.

When we experience a devastating loss—the death of a spouse or a child, a divorce, the bankruptcy of our business—it's tempting to make this wound the center of our story instead of one chapter. In the midst of our incredible pain, uncertainty and anger, we may feel as if our story has ended. We can't imagine picking up the plot of our lives again, turning a new page and continuing on with the same themes as before. And certainly, some events do change the plot, the theme and the pace of our life. But one thing remains the same no matter what happens.

We know how the story ends.

And as with the most satisfying novel we've ever read, it's a good—no, a *great*—ending. With God as the perfect author of our script, we know that He remains in control and that His love endures forever. We know that He will never abandon us. We know that we will be with Him always—even after our life on Earth has ended. We know that despite the limitations of our earthly vision, our Father is working out a grand narrative that revives, redeems and restores His children. In God's Word the process is explained this way:

> Blessed be the God and Father of our Lord Jesus Christ, who has blessed us in Christ with every spiritual blessing in the heavenly places, even as he chose us in him before the foundation of the world, that we should be holy and blameless before him. In love he predestined us for adoption as sons through Jesus Christ, according to the purpose of his will, to the praise of his glorious grace, with which he has blessed us in the Beloved. In him we have redemption through his blood, the forgiveness of our trespasses, according to the riches of his grace, which he lavished upon us, in all wisdom and insight making known to us the mystery of his will, according to his purpose, which he set forth in Christ as a plan for the fullness of time, to unite all things in him, things in heaven and things on earth.
>
> In him we have obtained an inheritance, having been predestined according to the purpose of him who works all things according to the counsel of his will, so that we who were the first to hope in Christ might be to the praise of his glory. In him you also, when you heard the word of truth, the gospel of your salvation, and believed in him, were sealed with the promised Holy Spirit, who is the guarantee of our inheritance until we acquire possession of it, to the praise of his glory (Eph. 1:3-14, *ESV*).

God created us in His own image, saved us through the gift of His precious Son and redeemed us for His glorious purposes. We can't always see what He's up to, but we can rest in the assurance of His promises. We can trust Him and His Word, even when our present reality seems contrary to this truth. And ultimately, we can know that we're part of something much bigger than our own lives. We're not just here to be happy or to enjoy a comfortable life, to struggle for that elusive dream of financial independence and early retirement.

No, we're here for God's purposes! He made us specifically the way we are and gave each of us a unique purpose. Only when we live out of this purpose can we experience real satisfaction and lasting joy. Circumstances do not dictate our access to peace, joy and abundant living—our faith in God does. When we share with others about the process of our responses, growth and faith in the midst of our trials and difficult circumstances, we model this kind of spiritual maturity to those who hear us. It's not that we have to act spiritually mature or pretend that we're not suffering—no, not at all. We simply have to allow God to be the power source for everything in our lives.

> For this reason, because I have heard of your faith in the Lord Jesus and your love toward all the saints, I do not cease to give thanks for you, remembering you in my prayers, that the God of our Lord Jesus Christ, the Father of glory, may give you the Spirit of wisdom and of revelation in the knowledge of him, having the eyes of your hearts enlightened, that you may know what is the hope to which he has called you, what are the riches of his glorious inheritance in the saints, and what is the immeasurable greatness of his power toward us who believe (Eph. 1:15-19, *ESV*).

Search and Rescue

Sharing our stories—telling the truth about what has happened to us and how that has made us feel—is a liberating experience. When we hold it inside, our pain festers into bitterness, rage and self-pity. When we release it, we experience cleansing and healing. And as we become whole again, our ability to share it brings the same power of healing to other people. It may also bring new insight to us and even give us greater awareness of God's continued presence in our lives. We rescue and encourage one another by sharing our stories.

The medical and psychiatric communities have learned what God's Word has always revealed: When we know the truth, speak the truth and live the reality of that truth, we are set free. Whether it's in AA, Celebrate Recovery, another addiction recovery program or therapy, the powerful release that comes from describing our experiences and sharing them with others can have a tremendous impact on our lives. However, for those of us committed to following Christ, this process is not about introspection, self-reflection or, worse, narcissistic navel gazing.

If we only tell our stories so that others will sympathize with, comfort and pay attention to us, then we're not moving through our pain but instead remaining imprisoned by it. It's only when we're able to release our pain to the power of our loving Father and share what He has done and is doing in our lives that our stories gain the real power of truth. I'm convinced that this is how we often realize that it's not all about us. When we reach out to others and relate our redemptive stories of God's power in our pain, we peek into eternity.

In other words, we heal ourselves and give honor to what God has done and is doing for us when we tell our stories. This is how our restoration echoes throughout time to reflect God's glory. As James explains,

> Brothers and sisters, as an example of patience in the face of suffering, take the prophets who spoke in the name of the Lord. As you know, we count as blessed those who have persevered. You have heard of Job's perseverance and have seen what the Lord finally brought about. The Lord is full of compassion and mercy. . . .
>
> My brothers and sisters, if one of you should wander from the truth and someone should bring that person back, remember this: Whoever turns a sinner from the error of their way will save them from death and cover over a multitude of sins (5:10-11,19-20).

James goes on to state here that our stories can even influence others to overcome temptation and avoid sin. Once again, this power ultimately comes from God, but when we see His power in action in another person's life, it strengthens us. We don't have to feel sorry for ourselves and remain mired in our emotional swampland. We can walk on solid ground if we follow God. With Him as our guide, we can recognize what we've lost as part of who we are but not as the defining part of our identity. We can experience the cleansing power of God's presence and allow the restoration process to proceed.

The Big Picture

God continues even today to use the healing and restoration that I've experienced to bless other people. One of the members of our church—I'll call him Bill—faced the sudden loss of his wife. They were both relatively young and had been married only a few years. While they were on vacation in Florida, Rebecca, his wife, started complaining of not feeling well. By the time they went to the hospital emergency room, her vital organs were beginning to shut down. Bill described the nightmare to me of helplessly watching his sweetheart slip into eternity. In a way, he had experienced circumstances similar to my own. In one moment, his life was changed forever.

Rebecca had always been very health conscious and appeared to be in great shape; however, tests revealed that all arteries to her heart were completely blocked.

Bill was beside himself. They had both believed in God and made Him the center of their relationship. They had enjoyed serving others and couldn't wait to have a houseful of kids of their own. And now Bill faced the loss of this beautiful, once vibrant woman.

I was privileged to walk with him through his wife's passing and the months of grief that followed for him. While I couldn't know exactly what he felt, I had a pretty good idea most of the time. Some days all I could do was listen with tears in my eyes, praying for him, hugging him, letting him know that God was still there for him.

I would never dare suggest that my friendship made Bill's pain any less bearable. Nothing I did or said could bring Rebecca back. But I do hope that somehow God used me to remind my brother in Christ that he was not alone.

Bill was familiar with my story of losing Debra and of meeting and marrying Cyd. Over time he asked me different details about that season of my life. He has told me that it helped him just to know that someone else had survived similar pain. It allowed him to keep his heart open to God and to vent his anger, hurt and confusion. It allowed him to take each day one at a time, trusting that somehow God would see him through it. After a year of grieving, God restored him by blessing him with another beautiful bride. While she could never replace Rebecca, Bill discovered a joy he once never thought would be possible for him again. God does not always restore what we've lost, but he always blesses us through our loss if we let Him.

This is the power that our stories can have when we allow God to use them.

Another recent instance comes to mind. Cyd and I were at a fancy party at a friend and professional colleague's home. Many successful people and even a few celebrities were there. As we mingled and got to know some of the other guests, we met a woman whom I'll call Sarah. She was alone and clearly distracted and upset. After we had moved through small talk, Sarah asked Cyd and me how we'd met. We looked at each other before smiling and proceeding to give Sarah the "short version" of us as a couple.

Visibly shaken, Sarah began to cry softly and said, "That is so beautiful—God—wow, He really must love you." Cyd and I tried to comfort her and told her that God loved her just as much as He loved the two of us. Sarah then began to confide about the painful state of her own marriage. She and her husband were barely speaking, and the fact that they would divorce seemed a foregone conclusion. We prayed with her and promised to continue praying for Sarah and her husband as they came to mind.

Almost a year later, Cyd and I were at another social event when a striking couple confidently approached us. The woman acted as though she knew us, but Cyd and I exchanged glances and raised our eyebrows, unable to place the faces of the man and woman.

Once the woman began to speak, recognition dawned for us both. You guessed it—Sarah and her husband! In short, she shared with us how they had started the process of reconciliation shortly after we had met her at the other party.

"I couldn't bear to think about losing him," she explained, "so I started asking God to help me—to help us both—quit being so selfish and petty. Dan here noticed a change in my attitude, and we started seeing a counselor and even going to church—and, well, here we are!"

Once again, my friend, Cyd and I had nothing to do with the way Sarah's marriage came back to life. Only God could have transformed their relationship to produce the loving couple we met that night. But we were grateful and humbled that God allowed our story to once more be a spark of hope to ignite the tinder of trust in someone else's life.

You may never know the outcome that God will bring about through the seeds planted by your own healing. Fortunately, He sometimes allows us a glimpse of how He uses our own restoration to restore others, but I suspect we often don't get to see the full impact. Maybe that's part of what awaits us in heaven—I don't know. But as we step back from our own little part of the painting and begin to see the entire mural spread out before us, I wouldn't be surprised.

RESTORE AND RENEW

1. If your life were made into a movie, what kind of film would it be? Drama? Tragedy? Romance? Comedy? Action adventure?

2. When have you been able to see God's bigger picture overlapping with key scenes from your own life? How has He reminded you that there's meaning and purpose even in the midst of your pain and suffering?

3. How have you been able to reach out to other people because of what you've been through? What new wisdom, strength and credibility have you gained as God continues to restore you?

4. Who comes to mind right now when you think of someone God wants you to minister to? What could you offer that person from your own experience of loss and restoration?

RECONNECT AND REVIVE

Father, my story would be meaningless without You as its author. Thank You for the way You unite the pieces of the chapters in my life with Your epic story of love and redemption. Please use me to reveal Your love, grace and redemption to others in need. Amen.

11

Persevere with Patience: Moving Forward with a Grateful Heart

Our church leaders had been in meetings for several hours when the sleet began to fall. Through the ranch-house windows, we could see chips of icy snow descending like crystal confetti, creating a picturesque scene straight out of a Thomas Kinkade painting. As beautiful as this scene was, it wasn't a welcome sight. I was at a leaders' retreat with our church executive team, our corporate board and other pastors at our church's ranch property in Whitesboro, Texas. Located a little over an hour from my home, the ranch offered the perfect setting for us to get away and look ahead to the new year and lift up prayers for guidance and direction to fulfill our ministry goals.

Earlier in the week the weather reports had warned of severe weather making its way to our region; we hadn't been sure what to believe, however, because the same predictions had been made two weeks earlier and had not materialized. So we had cautiously proceeded with plans for our retreat, knowing that we might have to postpone the retreat or cut it short, depending on the severity of the ice storm.

By the time we concluded the day's meetings, we were convinced that travel would now be treacherous. Looking through the picture-frame windows onto the small lake situated about 70 yards from the house, we realized that the sleet had become steadier. The storm had spread its white blanket across the surface of the rolling pastures surrounding us. Since more discussion and planning remained, we would continue our meeting the following day. Because of the developing weather, I decided to spend the night there at the warm, cozy ranch instead of driving home as planned.

Because I am a light sleeper, all through the night I heard the constant pinging of sleet on the tin-metal roof of the bunkhouse where I slept. The next morning's scene fulfilled the vision that forecasters had predicted: a coat of thick white ice layered the ground. Every tree branch, every evergreen, every tumbleweed glistened like a frozen landscape of blown glass. A beautiful display of winter beauty, the scene chilled me with worrisome questions.

Since meteorologists predicted more of the same, I began to wonder when I would get to return home and see my family. And more important, how were they faring in this winter wonderland? Was the power still on at home? Had Cyd gotten to the grocery store before the storm came? Would Seth and Caleb go stir crazy in the house and drive their mom up the wall? How long would the ice remain? I wasn't able to talk to them because cell coverage was already spotty at best in the Texas ranch country outside the Dallas-Fort Worth metroplex; the weather conditions didn't help either. The other impediment to placing a call home was our nonstop discussion—so by now I was even more worried.

Since our meetings concluded on the second day just before dinnertime, I decided to venture out onto the ice-covered roads to make my way home. I couldn't bear the thought of my family shivering without power or other necessities they might need. I didn't want to risk waiting another night, allowing another quarter-inch or more of ice to separate me from my wife and sons. Sure, I could have stayed at the ranch, but my gut instinct, divinely inspired, I'd like to believe, compelled me to attempt the drive home.

Time to Move

During a season of restoration, we sometimes must make hard choices not only about how to keep moving forward but also when to take the next steps. Obviously, many of the other pastors at the retreat felt as if they had no choice but to remain at the ranch. Perhaps it seemed like common sense to them to remain in the warm safety of the cozy ranch house. On the other hand, for me there was only one choice—not a logical or easy one—that brought a sense of peace. With my family's safety and comfort motivating me, as well as my desire to be with them, I knew what I had to do.

When my friend Keith had reintroduced me to my old college acquaintance Cyd, I had known what to do then as well. Sure, my heart had still been aching with loneliness and my healing had still felt fresh and fragile, but I'd realized that if I didn't at least call Cyd—you'll remember that I waited a couple months before finally dialing her number—then I would miss out on a blessing. Perhaps if I had known beyond a doubt that I wasn't ready to have a conversation of any kind with a new female friend, I wouldn't have made that call. Maybe if I had not found a level of sure-footedness on solid ground with the Lord, I wouldn't have felt strong enough to risk making that call, let alone going on a date shortly thereafter.

But as we advance through the process of healing and restoration, as we discover where God is leading us and what He has for us, it's important for us to remember three things. First, we want to make sure that our heart is aligned with God's timing and not stifled by the fearful snooze button that we might be using to keep us hiding under the covers. Once again, please remember that our emotions will distort, distract and disturb us if we let them. The trick is to express our feelings fully without letting them take over and control our decisions. God can handle our feelings and wants us to share our heart before Him. But we need to let Him, not the powerful feelings crashing inside us, be the force guiding us.

Next, we need to realize that God's timing will not necessarily make sense to those around us—and it doesn't have to. When we take each step through our season of recovery, our restoration relies on God and our obedience to Him, not on the approval or timetable of others. Someone going through a similar painful experience may move at an entirely different speed and take an entirely different route than we do. It's good to look to those who may have pushed through the kind of pain we're encountering, but we shouldn't expect our journey to look like theirs necessarily.

Finally, we must realize that the path ahead may be just as challenging as driving on an ice-covered road during the darkest winter night. Yes, there will be blessings along the way, confirmation that we're moving in the right direction, but things may not get any easier. Steps of restoration require us to exert all our strength possible in order to experience the fullness of healing.

It's like someone who breaks an ankle. Once the break has been examined and set, the person wears a cast until the bone starts to heal itself. But even when the fracture has fused the broken pieces into one bone again, the individual can't get up and run a marathon. No, this person has to take things easy at first, perhaps using crutches or a cane to prevent putting all his or her weight on the still-tender ankle. Physical therapy and rehabilitation come next and enable the person's ankle to regain the strength it once had. The ankle will never be exactly as it was before it was broken. But it can become strong and sturdy through gradual exercise over time.

The process of healing and restoration, just as in physical therapy, isn't easy and requires patience and perseverance, two qualities that God emphasizes repeatedly in His Word. We're told, "The testing of your faith develops perseverance. Perseverance must finish its work so that you may be mature and complete, not lacking anything" (Jas. 1:3-4). Apparently, we become more like Christ, more complete and whole, as we push forward and follow God.

And we will be rewarded for our hard work as well. "Let us not become weary in doing good, for at the proper time we will reap a harvest if we do not give up" (Gal. 6:9). Notice that it says "at the proper time"—not when we want it to happen and not when other people tell us, but in God's time. We grow impatient and tend to get stuck in the extremes, either charging ahead (or retreating) at our own speed or else staying put and refusing to move at all. Perseverance requires patience. Patience requires waiting on God. Waiting on God requires faith.

Committed to the Journey

That night, when I began the long, slow drive home along roads layered with close to an inch of ice in places, I definitely gained a new appreciation for patience. I figured that driving slowly, it might take me three or four hours to get home instead of the usual one and a quarter hours. It would be treacherous and slow going, but at least I would be with my family and get to sleep in my own bed.

Fortunately, I was not the only one eager to get home. Boy, was I glad when my friends and fellow colleagues Brian Coleman and Jim Mittan announced that they wanted to get home that night as well! Jim decided to ride with me; Brian would lead the way for us in his SUV, which had four-wheel drive. We quickly finished our dinners and started on our journey.

Mapping out our directions, we agreed to traverse west on Highway 82 to I-35 south. However, before we could even get to the road leading to the highway, which was only about a quarter-mile from the ranch, I had to face my first fear. In order to get from the ranch house to the front gate of the property, we would have to navigate the single-lane driveway that crossed over a small dam buttressing a lake located between the house and the public road. The driveway was already iced over, and a couple drivers who had ventured out earlier in the day hadn't been able to get their four-wheelers up the driveway incline. It didn't help matters when Jim mentioned that the lake was nearly 12 feet deep near the dam.

Inch by inch, following Brian's vehicle, he and I both somehow gained enough traction to make it to the end of the driveway. Whew—we had made it past the first hurdle! Conditions had definitely not improved, though. As we approached the ramp to Highway 82, we saw a truck careen into the four-foot-deep ditch as its driver hit black ice.

At that moment I seriously contemplated turning around, but Jim was on the phone talking with Brian in his vehicle ahead of us, and Brian had already entered the on-ramp to Highway 82. We were committed.

There was no way of knowing where the slick-as-glass icy spots were on the road. Traveling in the trenches made by the numerous vehicles that had already braved the treacherous conditions remained my first plan of action. The tires of my 5,200-pound Expedition began to spin, and the SUV's rear end began to slide to the right. I knew then that the best strategy was to drive on top of the trail of ice piled about four inches thick, which made for a very bumpy ride.

Traveling about 20 miles per hour, which almost seemed fast in those conditions, I looked in my rearview mirror to see the headlights of some yahoo fast approaching. I had been driving in the middle of the highway on top of the patchy ice and would have to move back into the ice-slicked grooves to let Mr. Hurry-up pass. Several very un-Christlike words came to my mind as the 4x4 Chevrolet passed me without seeming to care that he was endangering himself and others.

Glancing ahead, I spotted more trouble. As we approached our first upward incline, my stomach knotted even tighter, and my fists gripped the smooth leather of the steering wheel for dear life. Halfway up the hill, Jim asked, "How you doing?" I almost blurted, "Scared to death!" but I wanted to give my passenger full assurance that everything was under control, so I refrained.

Every once in a while, I could feel the tires spinning to get traction, which remained a constant concern. As we approached another hill higher than the first one, I gently pressed the accelerator, giving my vehicle more speed to make our ascent; to my amazement, it seemed as if the vehicle was being pushed from behind. I thought to myself, *The Lord has sent His angels to give us help*. The rest of the trek on Highway 82 to Gainesville, at the intersection for I-35, was uneventful, though my focus on the road was laser sharp and my stomach remained tightly wound. We weren't home yet, but we were making progress.

Deliverance from Distress

The journey of restoration not only requires patience and perseverance; it also requires courage from us to take the next steps and confidence that God will provide the way. It demands an awareness of God's perfect love that casts out our fears and overrides our imagination's worst-case scenarios. And it often means relying on the power of community to assist us on our journey.

While I would have made the trip by myself, it was somehow very comforting to have Jim and Brian with me. It not only made the experience less lonely, but it also provided concrete assistance if I were to get stuck, stranded or sideswiped. Jim and Brian wanted to get to their homes just as I wanted to reach mine. God brought us together and allowed us to travel that treacherous journey as a team instead of individually.

It's important for us to recognize when other people are traveling in the same direction we are. The encouragement that comes from knowing we are not alone explains why recovery groups, church community groups and prayer partners are so vitally important to restoration. Not only do the individuals in these groups often understand our pain, because we share similar struggles with them, but they also remind us that God often uses people to minister to one another in ways much more powerful than any we could come up with on our own.

When we stumble, or in my case skid, we know that we have someone to lean on, someone who will lift us up and make sure we don't remain stuck. Someone to give us real perspective: "Yes, this is really *hard*, and yes, *God is still here*, loving and guiding us." While these two statements may seem to pull us in different directions, ultimately they keep us moving forward. We acknowledge our feelings—I was scared to death driving on those icy roads—but we trust God and keep going with our divinely appointed destination in mind.

Perhaps no book in Scripture better expresses this reality better than Psalms. One of the many reasons that the songs in this book have such power and potency is their honesty. The poems here never shy away from the pain, disappointment and anguish of life, yet they never fail to draw our attention back to God and His character—to the fact that He loves us, rescues us, provides for us. Here's a good example from Psalm 107 of what I'm talking about:

> Oh give thanks to the LORD, for he is good, for his steadfast love endures forever! Let the redeemed of the Lord say so, whom he has redeemed from trouble and gathered in from the lands, from the east and from the west, from the north and from the south.
>
> Some wandered in desert wastes, finding no way to a city to dwell in; hungry and thirsty, their soul fainted within them. Then they cried to the LORD in their trouble, and he

delivered them from their distress. He led them by a straight way till they reached a city to dwell in. Let them thank the LORD for his steadfast love, for his wondrous works to the children of man! For he satisfies the longing soul, and the hungry soul he fills with good things (107:1-9, *ESV*).

These verses speak to the process of restoration. We often feel so aimless, so disoriented and confused by our pain that we can't find our way forward. We feel empty inside, hollowed out and beaten down, unsure of how anything good could come from our present loss. Consequently, we understand firsthand what it means for our souls to faint within us. We feel as if we don't have the energy, the spirit, the zeal for life that we need to carry on.

But notice this: It's when we feel overwhelmed that the tide turns, the Red Sea parts, the sick are healed and the tomb is rolled away: "Then they cried to the Lord in their trouble, and he delivered them from their distress." When we have nowhere else to turn or nothing else to lose, we can cry out to God. If we've already cried out, we need to keep crying!

Our Father hears us and will not ignore us. He may ask us to wait patiently or to take small, careful steps rather than the giant strides we would like to make. But He always hears us and cares about us. He will lead us in a "straight way" and satisfy our "longing soul." He will fill us with good things.

He *does* good because He *is* good.

You've Come Too Far

Notice too in these verses from Psalm 107 that we're told that God delivers us from our distress—not that He necessarily removes all obstacles from our path. Could the Lord have melted the road from the ranch back to my house? Of course! But that's not what He chose to do that night. He heard my prayers and delivered me from distress, but it still required some white-knuckled driving on my part.

Brian, Jim and I had made steady progress, but we still had a long way to go. As we approached I-35, we could see a long line of yellow taillights and red brake lights illuminating the southbound interstate. We got on the interstate, and traffic seemed to be moving at about 30 miles per hour; I was now feeling good about our decision to make a run for home.

Suddenly, though, we began to slow until we came to a crawl and then completely stopped. Jim reported that his wife, Susan, had texted earlier that she had heard I-35 south would be closed from 4 until 11 that night. We had not confirmed this to be true before we started our journey.

We were now in the thick of it all and moving at a snail's pace when I saw a truck veer to the right and cross a driveway from the interstate to the service road that ran parallel to the interstate. By the time Jim and I realized that this was a way out of the traffic jam, it was too late for us to inform Brian. However, we immediately saw another impromptu crossing lane between the interstate and the service road, which we were able to take. Once we got on the service road, we moved at a slightly faster pace and at the right time jumped back onto the interstate. But once again it wasn't long until we came to a complete stop.

We had been on the road for two hours now and had traveled little more than 25 miles of the 50 or more we needed to go. Traffic would move a few yards, then stop, a few yards, then stop, a few yards, then stop. We decided to try the service road again—this time blazing our own trail through the ditch and back onto the road. For a couple miles it seemed as if we had made the right decision. Then we came to the mother of all backups. We were trapped!

Nothing was moving—not on I-35 and certainly not on the service road. Jim's phone rang, and as he talked with his wife, the look on his face told me all I needed to know. Susan had informed him that the interstate was indeed shut down. Thoughts raced through my mind: *I should have stayed at the ranch huddled near a warm, cozy fireplace or a soft, comfy bed. I'm going to sleep in a cold, dark, icy SUV tonight. No hot food, no coffee, no bathroom—noooooo!*

Stopped completely on the service road, Brian joined Jim and me in my vehicle. I was glad that if I was going to spend the night in my SUV, I wouldn't have to do it alone. Over the span of the next two hours, we sat in the vehicle, hoping against hope that the interstate would reopen. Then something amazing happened.

Many drivers had passed us by, driving on the slopes of the ditch between the interstate and the service road; several times

Jim had wondered aloud how they were getting through the traffic jam and continuing on their way. Traffic on the interstate was not moving, although on occasion the service-road traffic would move a little and then come to a halt. Earlier I had seen in the distance cars making a right turn off the service road, but it was too dark to see where they were going. Jim located our position on his phone and discovered that those vehicles were taking an exit ramp that led to an overpass turnaround. If we got to that ramp, we could turn around and go north on I-35.

That led to discussion about heading back to the ranch, but I didn't give any thought to that. I heard the ol' James Cleveland gospel song playing in my head: "I don't feel no ways tiiiired, come too far from where I started from. Nooooobody told me that the road would be eeeasy; I don't believe He brought me this far to leeeeave me." However, maybe we wouldn't have to backtrack after all. Jim then noticed a route that we could take that would lead us to Highway 288 in Denton if we could indeed get to the turn-around overpass.

Maybe we would get home after all.

The Long Way Home

We had a new plan. It involved some backtracking, of course, but anything was better than sitting still. First things first, Brian queried whether our SUVs could traverse the ditch alongside the service road. Good question. He and I decided to go on a little scouting mission. The temperature was now about 27 degrees, and a bitter wind was gusting around 15 miles per hour. As we trekked toward the ramp about 100 yards away, I noticed a man crouched by the rear wheel of his 18-wheeler. It wasn't until Brian, who was walking to my left and closer to the trucker, began to profusely apologize that I realized we had invaded the trucker's private bathroom space. Talk about desperate times calling for desperate measures!

Finally at the ramp area, Brian went a little farther to see if we could cross a grassy knoll, because the service road and the ramp were completely blocked with traffic. By this time I was starting to shiver uncontrollably. Turning to head back to my SUV, the freezing north wind struck my face, and Brian and I began to run as best we could on the ice-packed grassy ditch. By the time I got back to the vehicle, my head felt frozen. As I climbed into the driver's seat, I gasped for breath and slumped toward Jim, yelling, "I'm gonna die! It's sooo cooollldddd!"

Jim and Brian laughed at my delirium just as traffic started moving. It was now after midnight. Five hours on the road.

We were in the left lane of the two-lane service road when the vehicles in our lane began to move to the left shoulder. As if on command, right before our eyes, a pathway opened up between those vehicles and a line of 18-wheelers that were parked to the right. The Red Sea had been parted, and we were on our way to the overpass turnaround!

Once over the overpass, with Brian driving in front of us and Jim giving him directions from his iPhone, we weaved our way through the ice-slicked back roads of the city of Sanger at about 10 to 15 miles per hour. I was amazed that after one in the morning a sand truck led the way through a portion of the road that we traveled. We finally arrived at Highway 288 in Denton at about two o'clock in the morning. It would be smooth sailing to our homes from here.

When we arrived in Denton, we all stopped so that Brian could get gas for his vehicle. As we reflected together on our seven-hour ordeal, on all that we had experienced and the choices that we had made, anyone watching us would have thought we had just scaled Mt. Everest. It wasn't Everest, but what we had experienced had created a memory of a lifetime. The journey hadn't been easy, and we probably wouldn't have started it if we'd known what we would face. But we'd kept going, and God had kept us safe.

We had taken the long way home and then some—but we had made it.

Jim later reflected on our triumphant expedition: "God is good. I was thinking today about the decisions God helped us make so we could get to the physical location on the access road and be able to get out of that jam. Several times we could have decided to stay on the highway, which only would have kept us stuck. How many times in our lives does the sum of several unknowingly related decisions put us in a position for God to ultimately set us free and into His blessing? And what does it take for Him to get us there, turn by turn?"

A New Arrival

Obviously, my seven-hour ordeal doesn't seem nearly as traumatic and dangerous now as it did at the time. And maybe my views were a little skewed by my fear, which may have resulted in my memories being exaggerated from what actually happened. But the sense of being on an adventure, on an odyssey toward home, remains with me as strong as ever. That's why I think that my little ice-skating session that night seems like such a good illustration of the potholes and pitfalls we face when trying to move forward in life. I believe this in part because Cyd and I have definitely navigated some events far more frightening than even the most treacherous winter's drive. Let me explain.

After Seth was born, it was almost two years before we were blessed to conceive another child. When Cyd and I became pregnant with our second child, we were elated to find out that this one too was a boy. Seth would have a playmate who would probably be rough and tough just like he was, a little brother to pick on as well as set an example for. We envisioned that they would be like two peas in a pod, dressed alike and inseparable.

Cyd experienced intense morning sickness, and when others told us that they would pray that her morning sickness would stop, we pleaded with them not to do that. Our research had revealed that the sicker a woman was during those first three months of pregnancy, the more viable the pregnancy. The sickness indicated that there were higher levels of hormones that would sustain the child in the womb.

So for the most part, Cyd's pregnancy with Caleb was completely different from her pregnancy experience with Seth.

On Friday, June 20, Cyd's contractions increased, and by early Saturday morning it was time for us to go to the hospital. Arriving around noon, this time Cyd knew the drill. There was no request for a burger and no fuss made about the luggage; she was very calm. As with her first pregnancy, she dilated very rapidly, and by two in the afternoon, contractions were steady. An hour later, however, the nurse checked Cyd and said, "We might have a problem."

She called the doctor in, who confirmed that the baby had had a bowel movement inside the womb. The doctor expressed to us his concern that if Caleb swallowed any of the fluid now in the womb, it would get into his lungs and could cause serious complications. After hearing his explanation, I felt as if an elephant had just sat on my chest. Trying not to let Cyd see my concern, I clasped her hand and said, "God is with us; don't be afraid."

Her eyes exposed her own worries in the fearful gaze she returned to me. As I moved away from the bed to place a phone call to Gordon Banks for prayer, all hell literally broke loose. Suddenly, several alarms sounded, and lights began to flash. As I turned toward Cyd, I saw the panicked look on her face just as the nurse rushed into the room. Cyd's bedside monitor revealed that her blood pressure was going up and that the baby's blood pressure was going down.

The delivery doctor and several nurses hastily entered the room. The doctor immediately took in the situation and yelled, "The baby's blood pressure is falling! Mom needs to be prepped for an emergency C-section."

Grabbing the doctor firmly by the arm, I asked, "What's wrong? What do you mean?"

He indicated that the baby's pressure was falling for one of two possible reasons: either he had ingested the toxic meconium discharged in his bowel movement (meconium is the official name of the bowel movement), or the umbilical cord had become twisted into a dangerous position around Caleb's neck. Either way, we faced a crisis. If something didn't happen quickly, Cyd was going to have a C-section. Our baby was in a fight for his life.

With the frantic pace of medical personnel in and out of the room and amid preparation for the surgery, Cyd spoke up. "I think I can push him out!"

Shocked, the doctor asked, "What did you say?"

"I don't want a C-section—I can push this baby out!" With that said, I looked into Cyd's eyes and saw a look of fierce determination that I had never seen before—she had the "eye of the tiger"—no, she had the entire force of a mama tiger fighting for her baby! Loudly screaming, she began to push with all her might as I gripped her hand and the doctor positioned himself for the delivery.

I prayed, "Lord, please don't let Caleb open his mouth for his first breath until he is outside the womb."

Cyd pushed about three more times with everything she could muster from her small frame; suddenly, the crown of Caleb's head appeared. The doctor grabbed his head and pulled it through the birth canal. There he was, our second-born son, with his eyes and mouth completely shut.

"Yes!" I shouted. Caleb had not taken his first breath, and my sweetheart had demonstrated great enormous strength and courage to bring him into the world. I was so relieved and so very proud of her! This time Cyd got a chance to hold the child immediately, before he was placed on the weighing table. We were so grateful for God's mercy and grace toward us.

Racing Toward Restoration

Neither of our pregnancies proved to be as easy or went as smoothly as we might have wanted. But with the birth of both our sons, God remained very present and used the hardships to reveal His glory. I shared some of the challenges of our first son's birth in chapter 9; however, what I did not share is that Cyd experienced complications after Seth's delivery that ended up having a great bearing on our second son's birth.

With Seth labor had lasted a long time, and he had crowned for two hours before entering our world. The delivery doctor, a partner from the practice where Cyd's usual doctor (who was on maternity leave, you may recall) worked, had arrived very late and performed an episiotomy without an anesthetic after Cyd's epidural had worn off.

Cyd had been released from the hospital with a low-grade fever that had climbed higher and higher each night, eventually leading to an emergency-room visit that had led to same-day re-admittance into the hospital. The culprit had been a staph infection in her left arm from the IV administered during labor and delivery. After two surgeries, a 10-day hospital stay, a scare that Seth might be infected, and five days of home-healthcare nurse visits, Cyd fully recovered.

Nonetheless, she was left with several ugly scars that continue to serve as a reminder of how the enemy had tried to take her out but how God had spared her life. During the ordeal her doctors had been concerned that she might lose her arm or, worse, that the infection had already spread all over her body. But by the grace of God, neither one of these had become a reality. Cyd and Seth had fully recovered. Only the scars remained, a tangible reminder of what Cyd overcame by the grace of God.

When Caleb came along, he brought his own excitement, as I just shared. However, there was one other interesting aspect to his delivery. The delivery doctor was the same man who had delivered Seth. Cyd's regular doctor was out of town this time, and this other doctor told us that he had been at the grocery store with a full cart of goods when he'd received the page about Cyd going into labor. Recognizing who we were and knowing that we had not received the best service the first time, he had immediately left his cart and rushed to the hospital, where he assured us that our second experience would be different from the first.

Honestly, Cyd especially was not pleased when she saw him, realizing that she had harbored unforgiveness toward him from Seth's delivery. However, God redeemed that first experience by giving this doctor another chance and giving Cyd a chance to forgive someone she had harbored resentment toward. In fact, when the doctor walked in the door, we knew that it was God's doing, because we had prayed that we would *not* get this man again. God clearly had something else in mind. Sure enough, our second baby's birth was a better experience as well as a moment of true restoration.

Having endured the challenges of the first pregnancy and delivery, Cyd was later battle tested. When faced with painful moments in our life, responding with patience, perseverance and praise will pay dividends in ways unseen. When God allows difficulties in our lives, only He understands how those obstacles prepare us for the future battles that will ultimately bring glory to His name.

Revelation 12:11 says that "we overcome by the blood of the Lamb and by the word of our testimony." Christ has done His part to honor the Father. We must do our part to submit to His process that will produce a testimony that will encourage those who hear the message of our victory.

Whether it's undergoing an arduous drive along icy roads or enduring the physical pains of childbirth and its aftermath, Cyd and I remain grateful for the things that God has allowed us to go through. When He orchestrates the plan for our lives, the experiences we go through prepare us to fulfill His purpose. The difficult seasons of our lives make us grateful when we prevail and triumph through our struggles.

We just have to take the next step.

RESTORE AND RENEW

1. When have you been stuck in place due to weather, traffic or other immediate factors beyond your control? How do you usually respond when you find yourself caught in such circumstances?

2. How have you been able to persevere through the process of restoration? What "speed bumps," or challenges, have slowed you down and proved most difficult to overcome? How has God sustained you through these times?

3. Who are the people who encourage you and inspire you to keep going? How does their example motivate you to persevere?

4. What fruits of perseverance have you experienced lately? How has God produced new growth and restoration in your life simply by the way you keep taking each next step?

5. What's your greatest need right now in order to continue to persevere and to seek God's healing? In addition to asking God to meet this need, find one other person you trust and ask him or her to lift up your request to the Lord as well.

RECONNECT AND REVIVE

Dear Lord, it's hard to keep going some days. I get stuck in place by old emotions, old habits and circumstances beyond my control. Remind me of Your sovereignty, and empower me to take the next step, day by day. Amen.

12

Connect with Community: Serving Others While Healing Your Heart

In chapter 8, I shared about the decision that Cyd and I made to allow our sons to play football. In fact, this past season I had the privilege of serving as an assistant coach to my son's fourth-grade team. This was the second year that this team played together. Since most of the boys had only learned to play tackle football the year before, it was amazing to watch them develop their skills as well as their ability to function as part of a team.

To make things fun, I gave each kid on the team a nickname: "Juggernaut," "The Train," "Thunder," "Lightning," "Braveheart," "The Boss," "Iron Man," "Tiger," "Overcomer," "Quickie," "Master Chief," "Airplane," "The Hulk," "Buckeye," "The Bear" and "The Lion." If these names sound less than flattering, please remember that this was a rough-and-rowdy group of boys wanting to be as tough, talented and tenacious as their favorite players on college and NFL teams.

While the names might not sound motivational, every boy seemed to love having some unique aspect of his character and ability brought to the foreground. Each one realized that he had something uniquely his own to contribute by virtue of his ability and the position he held on the team. Not everyone could be the quarterback or a tight end. Fans of the game know that a center, an offensive lineman and a great defensive back are just as important as the more prominent positions, even if they are not in the spotlight as much.

You see, my goal as a coach was not to get caught up in the *X*s and *O*s so much as it was to inspire these young men to achieve at their highest level—to give their best on and off the field.

Each boy was unique, and I enjoyed working with them all. But one young player particularly inspired me: Mitch. Mitch played defensive end, even though he didn't have the typical build for this position. He was not big and burly or tall and lanky; Mitch had a small frame, and he was thin. Nonetheless, he was opinionated and would tell others what was on his mind in a forthright yet kind manner. This kid could have been the poster boy for the saying, "It's not the size of the dog in the fight but the size of the fight in the dog!"

I'd never met a kid with a heart like Mitch's. Like the Energizer Bunny, he was determined to keep going and going and going. He loved football so much, especially tackle, that it never occurred to him to be afraid when facing boys 20 pounds heavier and many inches taller than himself.

Shortly after football season began—we were off to a good start—Mitch broke his hand in an accident off the field. His doctor's report confirmed that he would be forced to miss our entire season. As a team, we were devastated—what would we do without Mitch's fire and tenacity on the field? Where would Mitch direct his energy, now compounded by his loss and frustration? How would he respond to not being able to play with his buddies who had grown to count on him and he on them? And needless to say, how would his parents handle his reaction?

We would all find out at the very next game.

Everybody Counts

Before I finish Mitch's story and the way his response to a broken hand surprised us all, I want to pause and point out a couple of life lessons that I learned through this situation. First, there's nothing like a dozen 10-year-old boys to give a person perspective! Not that they wouldn't change during the remaining years until adulthood, but I felt as if I got a glimpse of their true characters and future selves when I watched them on the field. Those who were naturally bold and confident as well as the kids who seemed naturally shy and cautious captured my attention. The ones who relied on their size more than on their mind and vice versa. The ones who fit in easily as well as the loners looking for a place to belong.

As simple as it may seem, the same is true for us: Our Father created us just as uniquely as He did those boys on my son's team. And He created us this way in order for us to be part of a bigger team, a larger purpose, a grander story. Sometimes when we're struggling to heal from our losses, we lose sight of the way our gifts make a difference to those around us. During the process of restoration, we often become fixated on our own pain, frustration, anger and sense of loss. But at some point, it's time for us to return to the field and get back in the game.

Similarly, we must recognize our unique contribution and not compare ourselves to others nor underestimate the abilities and talents we've been entrusted with. God designed each of us for a specific purpose: to love and serve others as we advance our Father's kingdom. Although I'm pretty sure the apostle Paul never witnessed a group of boys chasing each other on a Texas football field, he describes our purpose this way:

> For just as the body is one and has many members, and all the members of the body, though many, are one body, so it is with Christ. For in one Spirit we were all baptized into one body—Jews or Greeks, slaves or free—and all were made to drink of one Spirit.
>
> For the body does not consist of one member but of many. If the foot should say, "Because I am not a hand, I do not belong to the body," that would not make it any less a part of the body. And if the ear should say, "Because I am not an eye, I do not belong to the body," that would not make it any less a part of the body. If the whole body were an eye, where would be the sense of hearing? If the whole body were an ear, where would be the sense of smell? But as it is, God arranged the members in the body, each one of

them, as he chose. If all were a single member, where would the body be? As it is, there are many parts, yet one body.

The eye cannot say to the hand, "I have no need of you," nor again the head to the feet, "I have no need of you." On the contrary, the parts of the body that seem to be weaker are indispensable, and on those parts of the body that we think less honorable we bestow the greater honor, and our unpresentable parts are treated with greater modesty, which our more presentable parts do not require. But God has so composed the body, giving greater honor to the part that lacked it, that there may be no division in the body, but that the members may have the same care for one another. If one member suffers, all suffer together; if one member is honored, all rejoice together.

Now you are the body of Christ and individually members of it. And God has appointed in the church first apostles, second prophets, third teachers, then miracles, then gifts of healing, helping, administrating, and various kinds of tongues. Are all apostles? Are all prophets? Are all teachers? Do all work miracles? Do all possess gifts of healing? Do all speak with tongues? Do all interpret? But earnestly desire the higher gifts (1 Cor. 12:12-31, *ESV*).

During the process of our restoration, we must remember two things: First, we must be willing to receive help and support from other parts of the Body while we recover. When we injure our physical body, the rest of our body naturally compensates for a period while the injury heals. When we sprain our ankle, one leg bears more weight than the other. When we break a finger on one hand, the other hand does more work.

Too often we try to detach ourselves from the rest of the Body of Christ and pretend that there's nothing anyone can do for us. While we may feel much pain and loneliness, these feelings will pass—and from my experience and that of others, they often pass more quickly when we share them with people who care about us and want to help us. Support during our time of restoration may come in the form of physical provision such as food, shelter, money or transportation. Or it may simply be the emotional support, the heart connection, the listening ear that sees us through. Or it may be a combination of both. Regardless of what it is, we have to accept support from other members of our Body.

A key part of our recovery, however, also involves knowing when it's time to return the blessing by serving others in need. Yes, there's usually a time when our loss may be the center of attention, but as we grow stronger, we must follow God's timing and be willing to give back based on what we've been given. If we cut ourselves off from the Body of Christ, we not only refuse to accept God's provision of assistance, but we also withhold the gifts that we could be giving in return.

When we isolate ourselves in our pain, we lose perspective on how many people love us, care about us and need our help. It's the lesson that George Bailey, Jimmy Stewart's character in *It's a Wonderful Life*, learns every year at Christmas time—and it gets me choked up with emotion almost every time. Each person leaves a void, a hole, when he or she withdraws and refuses to contribute his or her unique gifts to the world. God designs us for a purpose, and we only suffer more when we refuse to live out of this purpose. If we don't allow our test to become a testimony, then we miss out on true restoration.

Game Changer

The football team was going through pregame drills when I heard these words: "Hey, Coach!" As I turned toward the direction of the voice, there was Mitch, wearing his number 4 jersey. His face displayed an eager but nonchalant demeanor. I asked him how he was doing, and he told me that he was sad that he couldn't play but that it wouldn't stop him from cheering the team on and helping in any way he could. With that said, Mitch began to help us coaches retrieve balls and run drills with the other players. Mitch performed those duties with the same energy and tenacity that he used to chase down an opponent carrying a football—and it didn't stop there.

When the game began, Mitch stood on the sideline and cheered each teammate as he entered the field of play. He made sure that his teammates were encouraged when they came off the field and was waiting for them with a thirst-quenching burst of water sprayed from a plastic water bottle. Because of the Texas heat, the boys drank water like an unquenchable prairie fire. Mitch took it upon himself to refill the water bottles at the water fountain.

I marveled at the eagerness and energy with which Mitch worked to serve his teammates. Even though he could not participate in the game on the field, Mitch was no doubt in the game. This kid who was passionate about the game of football, after suffering an unfortunate incident, took a bad situation and turned it into something positive. All season long, game after game, Number 4 showed up and served his teammates and coaches with enthusiasm. Before the events of this season unfolded, I had known that Mitch was a great kid; but what I saw demonstrated over and over again each week revealed a champion.

Whether Mitch could have explained this truth about restoration, I don't know. But his actions spoke louder than any explanation he could have given. He refused to be sidelined, angry and bitter about what he had lost; instead, he was transformed by what he could find.

Give and Take

God's Word is clear about the necessity of God's people being in community and the mutual benefits of serving out of the relationships we develop there. Ecclesiastes declares that "two are better than one" (4:9). The Scripture proceeds to discuss the economic, emotional and physical benefit of having someone in our corner through the ups and downs in life. God has created us to be interdependent—not just on the receiving end but on the giving end as well. In this type of relationship, our strengths cover for our friends' weaknesses, and their strengths cover for our weaknesses.

Sometimes this interdependence goes off the rails and turns into dependency or codependency (you may have heard the old recovery buzzwords "dependency" and "codependency" before). When we lose equilibrium, healthy relationships often degenerate into unhealthy aversions to responsibility and equality. It's the shame and avoidance we see with Adam and Eve in the Garden of Eden after they disobeyed God and ate the forbidden fruit. It's the restless idolatry we witness in the people of Israel after God rescued them from bondage in Egypt. It's the exploitation and denial that we see today whenever we focus only on taking or only on giving.

Without getting on my soapbox, I think the following example illustrates this point quite clearly. Not long ago I had a conversation with a person who was in the throes of a financial crisis. It seemed that there was too much month left at the end of this individual's money! As I inquired about the source of his income, this person indicated that he was receiving a monthly check from the government. He went on to reveal the amount he made—"for doing nothing"—and I was shocked to learn that the check totaled less than he could have earned making minimum wage.

"You know you could make more money, right?" I offered. "Even a minimum-wage job pays more than you're currently getting."

"But I'll lose that check!" this person replied. "If I get a job, I'll lose the only steady income I have."

I thought for a moment. "So you'd rather keep receiving this check and remain stressed about money than work, earn twice as much and alleviate your financial strain."

It was clear from this person's response that he heard me but couldn't listen. From this conversation I realized that what had started out to be a good thing for this person eventually had become a bad thing. What had been designed to be a temporary hand-up had become a perpetual handout! Don't get me wrong—I believe that the government has a role in helping those less fortunate in our society. But the help should be a temporary transitional payment, not a lifestyle income. Personally, I believe that this role in which the government now functions became necessary when the Church, represented by the local community of believers, lost sight of the fact that we are to let our light shine so that God will be glorified (see Matt. 5:16).

There was a time when the church functioned as the social-relief program in our communities. Neighbors helped neighbors, and everyone pitched in to help those in the community who were caught in a tight spot. The beauty of this "I am my brother's keeper" concept was that those who needed assistance were also held accountable for the resources given them. If the resources weren't used for recovery and restoration, they were directed to someone else who would appreciate them and use the funds for the intended purpose.

During seasons of loss, crisis and rebuilding, most of us require assistance—the concrete kind as well as the intangible kind. However, when the hand-up eventually becomes a handout, the person on the receiving end becomes enslaved—dependent rather than interdependent. Sometimes we become so used to the role of grieving survivor or hurting victim that we forget who we really are. Restoration requires us to reestablish our role within our communities, finding the right balance again after losing ours temporarily.

Don't be the victim.

Be the victor.

Balancing Act

I understand that regaining our balance takes time. I was reminded of this while watching Nik Wallenda's tightrope walk across the Grand Canyon on the Discovery Channel. You would have thought that Nik was my brother and that I was standing beside Joel Osteen, praying along with him in suspense as he prayed with Nik before his walk. In between prayers I took deep breaths; the tension was almost too much to bear.

As Nik prayed and asked Jesus to calm the winds, I repeated his prayer, knowing the power we have as we agree together. Many thoughts raced through my mind as I contemplated what this man was attempting. *What possesses a person to attempt such a feat? What must his wife be feeling leading up to the moment her husband stepped onto the wire? How about his children? Are they gripped by fear or by faith? Is Nik courageously crazy or crazily courageous?* Obviously I had a hard time making the distinction!

Ultimately, though, I wouldn't call Nik crazy, especially knowing the meaning of that word. "Crazy" is defined as "mentally deranged, insane and impractical." The word conjures up thoughts of inappropriate, impulsive actions and reactions. It connotes a loss of control.

While willing to face factors beyond his control, Nik had done his homework and prepared in advance for this event. And despite the fact that he and he alone would be walking on that tightrope, it was clear that his action and the preparation for it was a team effort. The Discovery Channel did a superb job of explaining the extensive planning that Nik and his team had undergone to give Nik the greatest chance for success.

Engineers had calculated the proper use and mounting of the material and equipment to be used for the walk. Meteorologists had studied weather patterns and conditions. Nik had trained for over a year, simulating the conditions he would encounter during the suspenseful ordeal. Having taken care of the physical and practical conditions for optimum success, he had invited Pastor Joel Osteen to represent the spiritual component of the event. This extensive preparation would make one hard-pressed to call Nik crazy. I would call Nik courageous.

Courage is not the absence of fear but the management of it. Surely Nik was afraid as he thought about what would be required to walk across the canyon on a tightrope. As the moment arrived when he was to step onto that wire, his heart rate increased to a more rapid pace. In the middle of the journey, as the winds blew and the rocky slopes of the canyon walls and stabilizing wires created optical illusions, fear must have been Nik's constant companion.

He did not succumb to it, however; he simply managed it. He did not let fear define what he had passionately dreamed about all his life. He did not let fear rule his emotions and cause him to abort his lifetime dream. He calculated the risk and did not allow fear to deny him the reward of being the first and only man to ever walk across the Grand Canyon on a rope. He knew that he couldn't do it alone, even if he were the only one taking each step.

Maybe you don't feel as courageous as Nik Wallenda as you seek to regain your balance and return to your own tightrope across life's canyon of uncertainty. Perhaps fear has gotten the best of you and has stifled your productivity and stunned you into immobility. You may even know that you need help in order to get moving again, and yet you struggle to ask, receive and return the assistance that is available.

There is no doubt in my mind that you can accomplish the dreams that appear impossible to you—dreams that may have diminished due to your losses but have never died. If you're reading these words, then it's not too late.

You can make a difference in the life of those in your circle of influence; you can embark upon the journey of your lifetime, reaching heights that appear to be unobtainable. All you have to do is create a solid plan, surround yourself with skilled people to help you implement the plan, rehearse the plan and manage your fear. Nik's endeavor required planning, patience and participants and so will your restoration and recovery.

Maybe you know that you're not ready to get back on the tightrope and begin walking again. But even so, perhaps you can be like my old pal Mitch and support the rest of the team, giving what you can give, supporting others right where you are. I'm convinced that that's the real power of the Body of Christ, the real strength of true community.

Unity + Love = 13

Unity is one of the most powerful forces in all the earth. In fact, Jesus said in Matthew 18:19 that if two would come into agreement on Earth about anything they would ask, it would be done by our Father in heaven. Where there is agreement, there is power and peace. As I learned from my friend Rabbi Daniel Lapin, it is interesting to note that the Hebrew word for unity, *echad*, also has another meaning: a numerical value (as all Hebrew letters and words have) of 13, a number usually considered unlucky by most superstitious people.

If you think about it, our society goes to great lengths to avoid using the number 13. Most buildings and hotels do not have a thirteenth floor and neither do their elevators. People approach Friday the thirteenth with trepidation. Hard-core numerologists even postpone important tasks on this date. As Christians, we may scoff at such fallacies, yet we may have some of our own when it comes to our role in community.

Curiously enough, another Hebrew word with the same numerical value, 13, is *ahava*, which translates as the word "love." There can be no true unity where there is no love and no true love where there is not unity. These concepts working together and embraced by us can fulfill our restoration and extend healing to others as well. However, if we allow our pain to blind us, then we risk being as misguided as someone living by superstition. Although our suffering results from our losses and not from pagan customs or coincidence, we can still allow our fears to prevent us from experiencing the love, support and encouragement that come from true community.

When we allow others to help us, we experience benefits. But when we become willing to help others, we still experience blessings. We see that something positive can come from our heartache—that a seedling of hope has taken root and pushed through the soil of our desolation. If we're willing to serve others even amidst our anguish, God transforms our restoration into redemption.

Love in Action

Several years ago I learned a valuable lesson regarding a church's role in its community. Before a bank can receive a charter to serve a community, it must demonstrate to the banking commission how it will benefit the community. In the same way, there is no need for a church to exist unless that church is going to provide benefit to the community.

I have always believed that in order for our witness as Christians to be effective, our service to others, personally and in our community, must be practical. Jesus demonstrated the fact that when practical needs were met, ministry opportunity followed. When He healed the blind beggar, the beggar was prepared to follow Jesus wherever He would go. Because of that lesson and belief, I have initiated and participated in events that have helped people move to a deeper level of relationship with the Lord.

Community is both internal and external. When I speak of internal community, I mean the community within the church that has its foundation in small groups—even if it happens outside the four walls of the church.

I'll never forget my first experience being part of a church community group. I was 26 when I went to my first small-group meeting. It was anything but small, as there were about 30 people in attendance, and there was hardly any room to sit. I didn't know one person there except the small-group leader who had invited me. Toward the end of the meeting, we gathered in a circle; it was time to pray. I remember the leader speaking about the importance of transparency; if we were going to be a close-knit group, he said, we had to be willing to take our masks off. He went on and on for about 20 minutes, saying the same thing in different ways. I guess he was trying to get someone to muster up the nerve to share an area of need in his or her life.

As I looked around the circle, it seemed to me that everyone had their stuff together: Everyone was dressed nicely, they had all their teeth, they wore the latest designer shoes, and there was enough bling around their necks and on their fingers to open a gold-and-silver exchange store. I could tell by the awkward looks and the guilty stares at the floor that many wanted to say something. They wanted to confess that behind the got-it-together veneer, they didn't have it altogether and were exhausted from trying to pretend that all was well.

Being one who would rather take action than sit around talking about doing something, I decided I would break the ice. Because the small-group leader was still talking, I had to interrupt him to announce that I had a need and that everything was not okay. Not with me and not with my marriage.

The deafening silence was shattered by the stuttering of the small-group leader thanking me for being the first to step into the river of transparency. Little did I know that my actions would open the floodgate of prayer and forever change the dynamics of that small group. I decided then that I would do my best to lead others by being real about my own needs and not hiding behind the mask of protecting my reputation.

Purpose for Your Pain

The Lord has been faithful to allow my pain to find a purpose. As I went through the grieving process and remained transparent about the state of my emotions, many people came to me, inquiring about how I dealt with particular emotions. A man named Max, whom I had known for several years, reluctantly approached me one day after church. He had lost his wife to cancer. With tears in his eyes, he confessed to me that he would go into their closet, take hold of one of Samantha's dresses and smell the sweet fragrance of her perfume. He asked me, "Am I going crazy? Is that insane?"

Assuring him that he was not losing his mind, I shared with him that I had done the same thing after Debra's death every day for a few months. I had survived, and so would he. God is faithful to each and every one of us.

Years later, I was stunned by the intersection of my loss with another person's life. After sharing a message titled "Turning a Setback into a Step Up," I was approached by a guy who had made a decision to become a Christ follower a few years earlier. He shared with me that he could not believe his ears when I began to recount the events of the accident. He had actually been present on that fateful night.

John had lived in an apartment complex about 200 yards from the accident scene. His day that December 17 had been filled with mischief; he had been taking drugs, drinking alcohol and shoplifting.

He had been standing outside talking with his homeys when he'd heard a thunderous crash. Looking down the street, he had seen steam rising above the dimly lit streetlight. Surmising that someone had to be in serious trouble because of the horrific sound of crunching metal, he'd started running to the accident scene. When he'd arrived, he had seen me standing with a cell phone in my hand, talking, and then he'd heard me praying. As he'd peered into the passenger side of the car, he had seen Debra, slightly slumped over, bleeding profusely from her mouth.

At that time John had begun to question why he was even alive. He told me that he had been able to tell that we were good people, and he hadn't been able to make sense of why two innocent people would experience such tragedy while he, a lowly thug, was allowed to live. At that moment he'd made a decision that he had to get his life together. It had taken him two years before he'd made a commitment to Christ. Now here we were, 10 years after the accident, finally meeting. John thanked me for sharing my story and wanted me to know that his impetus to change had begun the night my world was turned upside down.

We never know the impact that our life's losses can have on another. God uses everything—even our worst moments—to redeem us and to advance His kingdom.

Pass It On

One of the ways I've witnessed the power of community comes from the Texada Foundation, a non-profit that Cyd and I established to provide educational alternatives to underprivileged kids and financial support to other non-profit organizations. There are many success stories related to scholarships that have been given away. One of my favorites involves a young man named Tommy who lived in a single-parent home. Because his mom was focused on providing resources to run the household, Tommy was practically on his own at 14 years old. To complicate matters, Tommy started following the wrong crowd.

Fearful that he would end up in jail or dead, his aunt decided to allow him to live with her. The foundation paid two years of tuition for Tommy to attend a private school; there he associated with other kids who were going in the right direction. Tommy graduated and joined the Army. He is now married and the proud, involved father of two kids.

Manuel was another kid whom we helped with a scholarship to a private Christian school. Manuel was fortunate to live in a home in which both parents worked. He wanted to attend a private Christian school because of the socially challenging environment of the neighborhood school. His parents, however, could not afford this. As a kid, whenever Manuel would come into my office, he would have me stand at attention and announce, "Ladies and gentlemen, the president of the United States!" Manuel is now in his third year of college and credits the Texada Foundation's investment in him as a key part of his success.

As I said, Christianity must be practical. There are two community stories that come to mind in this regard. We became aware of a lady named Janey who was a particularly faithful worker in her church. Janey suffered with a chronic disease that caused physical complications for her quite frequently. She had limited resources because she could not work a steady job, and her medical bills were too much for her to pay.

We were made aware that her home was in serious need of repair; in several places in the floor inside the home, the ground underneath the house could be seen through the floor boards that had rotted because of the numerous leaks in Janey's roof. Janey also used a cook plate to heat or prepare her meals, because her stove had quit working.

With a team of volunteers and some help from Lowe's, we performed a *total* makeover of Janey's home—the roof, flooring and appliances were replaced. A fresh coat of paint was applied to the exterior and interior of the house. Janey now lives in a comfortable, updated home generously supplied by those who sacrificed their time, talent and treasure to bring honor to God.

The other story that comes to mind involves our church partnering with a local non-profit organization that provides financial, emotional, medical and job-training resources in our community. Each summer businesses and churches partner with this organization to provide free lunches for children. Our volunteers from the church descend on a selected apartment community where the majority of the people are on Section 8 housing and living below the poverty line. Summer break for the children in the complex comes with mixed emotions. When school is in session, they have at least one good meal per day, but during the summer months many have to do without lunch. So we set up tables, make or purchase sandwiches, grill hamburgers and hotdogs, play games and set up bounce houses for one week.

We feed the kids a tasty meal and build relationship with them, letting them know that the Lord loves them. Many have made decisions to become Christ followers.

One time we noticed that for several of the days, one of the kids, Mario, didn't wear shoes when he came to eat lunch. One of the volunteers was really concerned about him and inquired as to the whereabouts of his shoes. Mario's sister told the volunteer that her brother didn't have any shoes to wear. Before the day was over, through the generosity of volunteers who had overheard the conversation, little Mario had several pairs of shoes. You should have seen how proud he was when he came walking into the dining area with his new white tennis shoes.

I share these examples with you not out of pride or false humility (another form of pride), but only to glorify God and demonstrate the way my life's most tragic loss has become a part of my legacy. So many people have helped me and Cyd get through the painful seasons in our lives. From the loving-kindness of friends and family to the gracious generosity of strangers, we know that God loves us through other people. Similarly, we find true joy in ministering to other people because of the dramatic gift of God's grace that we've received in our own lives.

Regardless of the losses in your life, you too can know the healing power of community. When we've suffered in our lives, it's tempting to isolate ourselves through self-pity, detachment, anger and resentment. But the key to seeing God move in our lives is often found in our relationships with other people as we serve and give of ourselves to address their needs. In fact, we're helping ourselves through our pain the most when we serve other people.

RESTORE AND RENEW

1. How has God uniquely equipped you to serve others? How have your losses, weaknesses and injuries influenced your ability to serve others in need? How would you respond to others going through the kind of painful circumstances that you have already experienced?

2. What areas of service to the Body of Christ bring you the greatest joy? Who needs you the most right now to serve him or her with your gifts?

3. How have you experienced healing and restoration through the process of serving others? What has God revealed to you about Himself through your willingness to focus on the needs of others more than on your own pain?

4. What has God shown you through the process of reading this book and allowing Him to restore you? How are you different now than when you started this book?

5. How will you respond differently the next time you experience a painful setback, a devastating disappointment or an unexpected loss? How has your attitude toward God changed most recently?

RECONNECT AND REVIVE

Heavenly Father, I love You so much and give You thanks and praise for all the amazing things You're doing in my life. Thank You for the ways You've revealed Yourself to me—even through this book and through Ricky's story. Please allow me to bless those around me by serving them with a sense of humility, strength and grace. I'm so grateful for the way that You continue to transform my breaking points into turning points of grace and redemption. You are an incredible God, and I will continue to trust You with all my heart! Amen.

Conclusion

Plan to Prosper

You won't live past 25 years old.

Strangely enough, this thought frequently ran through my head when I was a little boy. The seed for this inaccurate (thank You, Lord!) prediction came from a popular song at the time, "Only the Good Die Young." As I got older, I realized that the song is about a guy trying to get a nice Catholic girl to "go all the way" with him. But as an elementary school-aged kid, I couldn't grasp anything beyond Billy Joel's title and catchy refrain.

Most fascinating of all is that I perceived myself to be "good"—which apparently posed a threat to my young life. I was frequently told that I was a good boy, and I tried to be helpful and to treat others the way I wanted to be treated. I would help Pop and Aunt Too Sweet, my great-uncle and -aunt, as you'll recall, with household chores and yard work—without them asking and without expecting anything in return. I loved going to church and was careful to tell the truth most of the time.

Let's Make a Deal

With this evidence to back up my moral character, I perceived myself as good, haunted by my seemingly inevitable fate, at least according to America's Top 40 Countdown. Still occasionally haunted by the voice of Billy Joel, at 16 I made a vow to God: "If You help me get a starting position on the football team, I'll give my life to You at the end of football season my senior year. I will never play organized football after that." I don't recommend bargaining with God, but He is merciful and kind and didn't seem to hold it against me in my youthful sincerity.

Miraculously, I got a starting position the very next day. The defensive coordinator told all the starting cornerbacks and safeties that they were done because of their poor tackling techniques during the drills. I started as a defensive back for two years.

I remember the last game of my senior year. We were playing our crosstown rival, the Bolton Bears, whom we hated passionately, and I had not lost to them in the three previous years. It was a defensive battle. As the game clock wound down to the final minutes of the fourth quarter, we held a 13-7 lead. However, the Bears, through a combination of running and passing, had driven the length of the football field, and the ball now rested on the eight-yard line, first and goal.

We managed to stuff three running plays, and the Bears had no option but to go for the touchdown to tie the game. The quarterback, with his hands under the center, called out his cadence, looking from his left to his right. Several thousand fans in the stands were yelling at the top of their lungs; however, the intensity of my focus on keeping Bolton from scoring drowned them out. The center hiked the ball, and the quarterback dropped straight back to pass. I was playing left cornerback and was covering my zone when through my peripheral vision, I saw a receiver breaking toward the middle of the end zone. The quarterback's eyes were set on him as the target. I broke from my coverage on the left side of the field and made a frantic dash toward the middle of the field.

Everything appeared to move in slow motion now. The quarterback cocked his arm back, preparing to throw to his target, now standing in the middle of the end zone. When the QB released the ball, I dove toward the receiver with my body now horizontal to the ground. Just as the ball was about to hit the fingers of the Bear's receiver, the tip of my middle finger made contact with the ball. The ball was deflected to the right and fell harmlessly to the ground. We had secured the victory, our fans went crazy, and my teammates and I celebrated wildly.

And yet there was one voice that stood out above the rest that night. As I walked out of the end zone after the game, I heard, "Time's up!" It was the Lord now coming to collect on the vow that I had made two years earlier. I wanted to serve Him as I had promised, but I couldn't imagine myself as some kind of pastor or

Bible student. What had I been thinking to make such a promise to the Lord?

Fresh Start

After the football season was over, my coach inquired as to whether I wanted to play football in college; he assured me that he could get me a scholarship. I told him that I wasn't really interested in playing football in college. While I had no real intention of serving the Lord as I had vowed, I had enough fear of the Lord that I thought to myself, *If I play college ball, I might end up with a broken neck.* After that time I began to make some of the worst moral decisions I had ever made, and my awareness of God's presence in my life began to wane.

As I prepared to go to college, the thought of not having to live at home or go to church was quite appealing. Finally I'd be free to live life the way I wanted to live it, with no constraints and no one standing over my shoulder calling me into accountability for my actions. I determined that I would accomplish three objectives in college: get an education, sleep with lots of girls, and party and then party some more.

Once on campus, I found the perfect role model for my new objectives. My oldest brother, Greg, had been my hero; I had always idolized him because he marched to his own drumbeat. He was not swayed by peer pressure and was well respected by everyone who knew him—or so I thought. Then I saw the real Greg during my first three days on campus. He was living my three objectives to the max.

But when I realized this, I also realized that I didn't want to live that way. So I reframed my personal goals. I would get my education, sleep with only one or two young ladies, and only party occasionally. All things in moderation, right? This was my plan, but soon I would find out that God had a different plan.

If I was going to implement action items two and three of my plan, I would have to attend the first party on campus, held in the student union. When I walked through the doors, I felt confident that tonight was going to be my lucky night. I asked a young lady whom I had met just a few days earlier if she wanted to dance; she accepted the invitation, and we were on the dance floor in a split second. Finally I was cutting loose and enjoying myself. Thoughts of Greg, God and Billy Joel were the furthest things from my mind!

When the Music Stops

The music was rocking, the lights were flashing, the atmosphere was invigorating—but suddenly I knew something was very different. The proverbial music stopped playing. God invaded my space, and a question came to my mind: *What are you doing here?* It was not a question concerning my physical location but one regarding my purpose, my reason for being and the way I was living.

The question didn't come by God's audible voice; nevertheless, I recognized that it was the Lord speaking to me. I was surrounded by people who appeared to be having a good time, yet I was so alone—so naked. Startled by the sudden change in atmosphere, I said to the young lady, "I have to go." I couldn't explain what had just happened to me, so I simply left the party.

The walk back to the dormitory was only about 10 minutes, and during that time I called out to God, "Lord, I'm not sure You exist. Mom and Dad say You do, but I'm not sure. I know I have grown up in church all my life, but I'm not sure You are real. If You are, then make Yourself known. If You don't, I'm going to get my education, sleep with girls and party."

Over the next several weeks I was haunted by that question: "What are you doing here?" Looking back now, I can see how the Lord began to orchestrate relationships for me so that I would be introduced to Him. One such relationship was with a man named Paul Abrams.

Paul Abrams was the director of the freshman dormitory Jones Hall. Prior to arriving on campus for the freshman orientation, Greg had warned me to stay away from "Dean Abrams." His instruction concerning Dean was based upon the fact that Dean Abrams had served in Vietnam during the Vietnam War.

Another reason given by Greg was that Dean always sat behind his desk reading the Bible; as he read, his lips moved as if he were speaking; however, no sound came out of Dean. Because of the nagging question about my purpose, I was now on a mission to discover it. Dean's dedication and consistency caught my attention. Because of that, I would start conversations just to see where he was coming from spiritually. After a few conversations he invited me to his church, Bethany Baptist Church, pastored by Roy Stockstill (who would eventually turn the reigns over to his son, Larry Stockstill). Bethany was located in Baker, Louisiana, a small town just to the north of Baton Rouge. When we arrived at the church, I was fascinated by the size of the building; it was the largest church structure that I had ever seen that didn't look like a church. It was just a large, square, sheet-metal building. At that time it had over 2,000 members. I noted that the parking lot was full, which I found odd, especially for a Wednesday night service. When we entered the building, I saw that the place was packed from wall to wall with people, and the usher politely asked us to wait for a moment until he could find us a seat. What I'm going to describe now happened in what seemed like only a 20- to 30-second wait.

Standing and waiting to be seated gave me time to observe what was happening around me. We had walked in during the singing part of the service, but what caught my attention first was the racial diversity of the church. Every race was represented in that congregation, and people of every color were standing and singing next to one another, not in divided sections grouped by race. My second observation focused not on the song being sung but on the presentation of the song itself. People sung as if Jesus were standing right there on the stage; they were singing to Him. They weren't singing about Him or about their own struggles. *They're singing to the Lord as if He is standing onstage*, I thought to myself.

That was the first time in my life that I realized Christianity was about a relationship and not about religion. My third and final observation made me more curious than the first two. The congregation burst into spontaneous worship, but I couldn't make out what they were saying, so I leaned in toward the audience. There was a beautiful melody and harmony flowing from the mouths of the worshipers; I realized that they were not speaking in English. *What is this sound?* I asked myself. *It's the most beautiful sound I have ever heard—it sounds like angels are singing!* At that moment the usher appeared, informing me that he had a place for us to sit. As we walked down the aisle, I thought to myself, *I don't know what these people have, but whatever it is, I want it!* I gave my heart to the Lord that day.

Funny thing, Greg watched me for six months after I attended that church service and gave my life to Christ, and then he decided that he wanted some of the same thing too! He not only became a fellow believer, but Greg also became a fellow pastor. He leads an exemplary life and is an outstanding pastor. Today he ministers in the town where we were raised: Alexandria, Louisiana. In fact, all five of my brothers and both of my sisters as well as all 20 of my nieces and nephews know and love the Lord and serve Him in various ways with their many gifts. The impact on my family wasn't because of anything I did, but it had everything to do with what God continues to do in people's lives around the world.

A Hope and a Future

After I gave my heart to the Lord, it became very clear that lyrics from a pop song could not define my life expectancy or my future. I had a new song in my heart, one with an eternal message of hope and joy. Without a doubt, I realized that the times and seasons of my life were in the hands of the One who made me. I knew that the Lord had plans for my life—plans to prosper me, not to harm me, plans to give me a hope for my future.

Just as He did with me, so too God has an intended outcome for your life. He is the great architect, the originator of all things, who has "plans to prosper you and not to harm you, plans to give you hope and a future" (Jer. 29:11). Even if we don't always understand the process, He knows the plans that He has designed specifically for you—but trust in Him is paramount!

What I had to endure is not what you will have to endure or vice versa. Each plan is tailor made and fits each of us like a fine customized garment. Although I've communicated some deep struggles, I pray that this book has brought joy to your heart and hope to your healing process. Perhaps you've experienced a range of emotions regarding my account of how God has moved in my life and turned my mourning into dancing. Whether you see signs of it yet or not, you must know that He is doing the same for you! I want you to know that there is nothing special about me that God would favor me so much. He simply had a plan that was especially prepared according to His desired outcome for me.

As you reflect on the story of my life and on the truths God has revealed to me, I leave you with this:

1. *Trust God!* You can trust Him because He loves you so much. How do we know this? First of all, His Word tells us so over and over again. Second, and most important, He gave His only Son, whom He loves so much, over to a tragic death for us in order to prove that He loves us just as much as He loves Jesus.

2. *Never give up!* Quitting is the easiest thing to do and should never be an option. There will be a day for all who are in Christ when we will cease from the troubles of this world and find an everlasting place of peace. This world is not our home but only a temporary assignment. Remember that we are pilgrims and strangers passing through this land. Strength and perseverance take courage. Just take each hour, each day, each moment as it comes, leaning into the Lord and taking the next step.

3. *Make the exchange with God!* Acknowledge your pain and your feelings. Give them over to Him by laying your fears, doubts, failures, emotions and heart at the foot of the cross. Receive His love and incredible grace. Ask for help and receive His provision for you. Wait on Him by reading His Word, praying or worshiping. Let Him remove your pain through His own process and timing, because nothing and no one else can.

4. *Keep moving forward!* In your world as well as in your perspective, everything has changed. In the Lord's world and from His perspective, nothing has changed. His plan for you is on schedule and right on time. He is never out of control! But we must relinquish control of our lives to Him. Trust that He can do what He has promised to do, and keep moving forward, inch by inch, moment by moment, mile by mile.

It's hard to hope when someone we love leaves us or when life deals us a crippling blow. It's hard to trust God when the expectations we have built on following Him seem to take us through a minefield of pain, anger and sorrow. But as I've shared within these pages, God *is* faithful. He loves us, and His plans for us are for good. Even when others may intend to harm us, God uses terrible events for our good.

With a loving Father leading us, we experience the freedom to hope, the joy to live with purpose, and the peace to overcome the pain of the past. This is what remains true and real, no matter what you may be going through. Thank you for sharing this journey with me. My final prayer for you is the same timeless blessing we find in God's Word: "May the LORD bless you and protect you. May the LORD smile on you and be gracious to you. May the LORD show you his favor and give you his peace" (Num. 6:24-26, *NLT*). Amen and amen.

As you complete your own journey of restoration, Godspeed, my friend!

Acknowledgments

There are so many people that the Lord placed in my life to help me become the man I am today. This book would not have been possible without their love, patience, wisdom and faith.

To my mom and dad: Thank you for the vision you had for your children. Though you never left the little community affectionately called "the bayou," you inspired us to dream. You taught me to keep God first and said that I could accomplish anything my heart desired through discipline, hard work and acceptance of personal responsibility. Dad, you showed me by your lifestyle how to be a man of character. Mom, your faith and constant prayer demonstrated to me that God is real.

To the love of my life, Cyd: You are my double portion. When my future was erased and all hope seemed lost, the Lord injected you into my life. You came out of nowhere—feisty, classy, intelligent and a priceless treasure from the throne of God. You have inspired, encouraged and challenged me to never give up on life. You are my warrior princess!

To Pastors Mike and Kathy Hayes, my spiritual parents, mentors and friends: You were a part of my restoration of faith in pastors. You have encouraged me, been patient with me and given me ministry responsibilities and opportunities that allowed me to mature into a principled leader. Words are inadequate to describe the level of respect and love I have for you. We are in Covenant forever!

To Jan Miller-Rich and the Dupree/Miller team, Shannon Marven, Lacy Lynch, Ivonne, and Nikki: I thank you for encouraging and believing in me throughout this writing process. My thanks go to Dudley Delffs for your creativity and insight. Thank you to Kim Bangs and team, Tasha Ruffing, Jackie Medina, Carol Eide, Julie Carobini and Rob Williams. A job well done! Thank you to the Bethany House team. Our journey begins . . .

About the Author

Ricky Texada serves with his wife, Cyd, as pastor of Covenant Church in Colleyville, Texas, one of the four Covenant Church campuses in the Dallas/ Fort Worth area. The Texadas have led this campus since its inception in 2006 (www.covenantchurch.org). Covenant Church is a dynamic, thriving church, founded by Pastors Mike and Kathy Hayes. It has an average weekly attendance of 7500+ at four campuses in the Dallas/Fort Worth Metroplex and one in Flagstaff, Arizona. Covenant Church produces *Covenant Radio*, an internet radio program of praise and worship and excerpts of teaching from different pastors. Excerpts from Ricky's messages can be heard at covradio.org.

Covenant also has a network of affiliate churches and ministries in the U.S. and abroad. This international affiliate network is a relationship-based network of churches and ministries that are united in building great churches together and transforming the church experience for millions globally. Their model includes building strong families, building strong churches through modeling and mentoring, and building the Kingdom through expansion into the gateway cities of the world.

In addition to their influential pastoral work, Ricky serves as a board member for Covenant Church and Makeaway Charities—a non-profit established to make a difference in the lives of individuals and communities by providing short-term financial assistance to prevent long-term financial catastrophes.

Throughout his 20 years of ministry, Ricky has challenged and inspired thousands around the globe to pursue a deeper walk with Christ. Ricky and Cyd share an incredible testimony of God's faithfulness in the midst of tragedy and difficult circumstances. Theirs is a story which highlights God's grace, mercy and restoration power for those who are willing to place their hope and trust completely in Him. They are the parents of two sons. You can read more about Ricky and follow his blog at Rickytexada.com.

DEVOTIONS FOR EVERY DAY OF THE YEAR

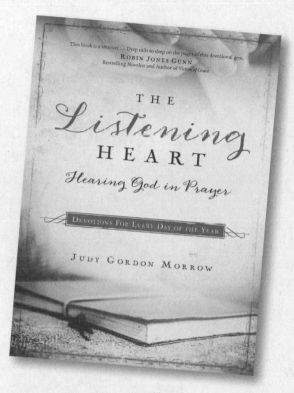

More. Life is full to overflowing, but we crave an illusive more. Via social networking, airwaves, and TV, our culture tells us to strive for more stuff, more activities, more adventure—you name it. Yet we are often left unfulfilled and wanting. Empty, even. With so many demands for our attention, it is difficult to quiet our minds long enough to hear the still, small voice of our loving Father, and to listen to the One who desires to bring us so much more than the noise of everyday life.

Judy Gordon Morrow discovered the *more* when her world was turned upside down and she knelt before God to seek Him and ask for His help. More than a decade ago, in tear-stained notebooks, she began to pen God's responses to her desperate prayers. Now, in *The Listening Heart*, Judy invites you to spend a year hearing from the God Who Speaks—the God who wants to speak to you. Each daily devotion echoes the Father's love and care for you, offering hope, comfort, encouragement and more—a rich closeness with God that will satisfy the longings of your heart.

The Listening Heart
Judy Gordon Morrow
978.07642.15261

Place Your Trials in God's Hands

Are the bills stacking up while your bank account dwindles? Is your marriage or your singleness a source of heartbreak? Are you filled with anxiety because of health issues? Do you sometimes feel like you're drowning and God is nowhere to be found? Do you wonder, *What in the world am I going to do? How am I going to make it?*

Trials roll in like waves, one after another, and threaten to knock you off your feet. But instead of trying to stand strong against your problems, maybe the answer is to be swept away—not by your troubles, but by God. *Overwhelmed by God and Not Your Troubles* is an invitation to rest and to fall into God's love, goodness, grace and forgiveness. Lift your tired eyes from the crushing trials that lead you to despair and fix your eyes on the awesome power and mercy of the God who is greater. You will experience the peace, contentment and joy that can only be found in Christ as you face your setbacks and heartaches with renewed hope and strength from the Spirit.

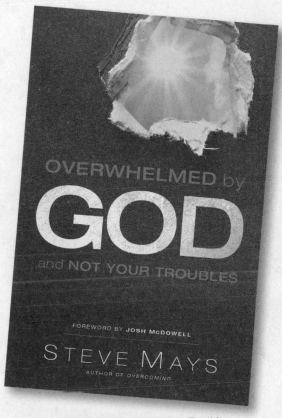

Overwhelmed by God and Not Your Troubles
Steve Mays
978.07642.15124

Available wherever books are sold!

BETHANYHOUSE

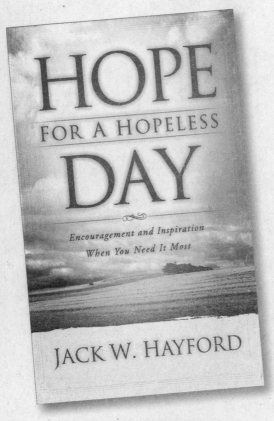